BEADWORK Creates
JEWELRY

BEADWORK® Creates
JEWELRY

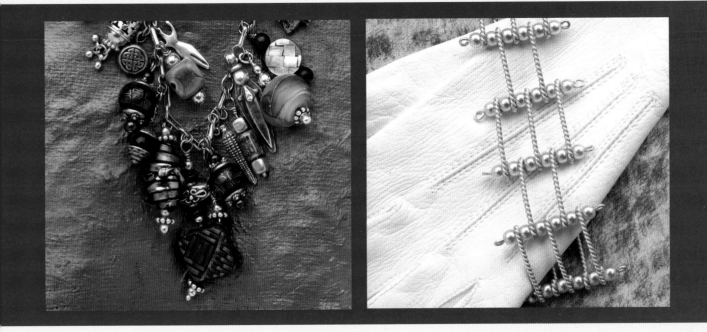

40 Beaded Designs

Jean Campbell

INTERWEAVE PRESS.

Interweave Press LLC
201 East Fourth Street
Loveland, CO 80537-5655 USA
www.interweave.com

Printed in China through Asia Pacific Offset

Library of Congress Cataloging-in-Publication Data

Beadwork creates jewelry : 40 beaded designs / Jean Campbell, editor.
     p. cm.
  Includes index.
  ISBN-13: 978-1-59668-037-1 (pbk.)
  ISBN-10: 1-59668-037-7 (pbk.)
  1. Beadwork--Patterns. 2. Jewelry making. I. Campbell, Jean, 1964-
  TT860.B3364 2007
  745.594'2—dc22

                              2006024455

10 9 8 7 6 5 4 3 2 1

{Introduction}

In that famous movie, Marilyn extolled the virtue of diamonds. And I guess Liz thinks they're a girl's best friend, too. But for me, a tray full of semiprecious stone, precious metal, crystal, and handmade beads has so much more meaning, creative potential, and often just as much beauty. Quite simply, it's difficult to escape the allure of beads. They can make a person delighted and dumbfounded at the same time. Their sparkle and dazzle have a Svengali-like effect, drawing you in. And once you start putting them together, there's no turning back.

Beadwork Creates Jewelry features forty of the best beaded jewelry projects you'll ever find between two covers, and will quickly entice you to jump into the beading fray. These crème-de-la-crème pieces were selected from four of the *Beadwork Creates* series, a set of six books, each showcasing a different type of accessory. *Beadwork Creates Earrings, Beadwork Creates Bracelets, Beadwork Creates Necklaces,* and *Beadwork Creates Rings* each contain some pretty amazing projects, let me tell you. I know, because as editor of all of them, I searched high and low to find the very best! The books have been extremely popular in the United States and abroad, and they've even been translated into Russian (just call me Джцн Кэмпбелл!). Their popularity is rightly so, because all the pieces come from top-notch designers and all remain drop-dead gorgeous.

The pieces you see in *Beadwork Creates Jewelry* aren't only beautiful to look at and wear, they are also really fun to make. You don't need to be a pro to create them—just curious to learn. The dozens of techniques included read like a laundry list of beadwork standards but include some pretty novel ones, too. They cover stitching with needle and thread, working wire with pliers, simply sliding beads onto a string, and more. When you pair all those great beading techniques with designer bead choices, the result is a visual feast of what the world of beads has to offer.

Treat this book much like a jewelry shop window. Stroll on by and pick your favorites. As is often the case when walking past Neiman Marcus, Barney's, Fred Segal, or Harrods, you'll certainly find several pieces you can't do without. (Perhaps those pieces resemble jewelry found in those famous shops?) The next step is to visit your local bead store and use the projects' materials lists as your shopping guide. Review the Techniques section on page 119 to learn or brush up on beading basics. Then belly up to the table and get to work. Before you know it, you'll find yourself back in the bead shop to make your next project. It won't be long until you have a jewelry box filled with pieces you only dreamt of owning before now.

So enjoy bringing those sparkling dreams to reality. It's not too hard to do when it comes to beading. And if you become seduced as I am, you might find that diamonds aren't a girl's only best friend.

Happy beading,

Jean Campbell

{Contents}

Earrings

Rings

Elizabethan Cuff

Donna Anderson Swiderek

Use bugle beads to make a three-dimensional right-angle weave matrix, and then embellish it with pearls, crystals, and seed beads. The result is a spectacular bracelet even Queen Elizabeth would find hard not to wear.

Materials

5 g charlottes

5 g Delica beads

Size 1 Japanese bugles

174 Swarovski crystal 4mm bicones and/or 4mm pearls

3-hole clasp

Power Pro, Silamide, or Size D Nymo beading thread

Tools

Size 12 beading needle

Scissors (or children's Fiskars scissors for the Power Pro)

Tape measure

Technique

Right-angle weave

See pages 119–125 for how-to

1 Measure your wrist and add ½" (1.3 cm). Measure the length of the clasp and subtract that figure from the previous measurement.

2 Use 6' (180 cm) of thread to string 4 bugles, leaving a 4" (10 cm) tail. Tie a knot to form a circle and pass through the next bugle to hide the knot. Don't weave through the beads again.

3 Use bugles to work a strip of right-angle weave that is 5 rows wide and the length determined in Step 1.

4 Fold Row 5 at a 90-degree angle from the rest of the beadwork. This will be one of the side "walls" of the bracelet. String 2 bugles, pass through the adjacent vertical bugle of Row 4, and pass through the vertical bugle of Row 5 and the bugle just strung so you make a square that sits at a 90-degree angle from the rest of the beadwork. Repeat for Row 3 (Figure 1). Fold Row 1 up to match Row 5. String 1 bugle and make a right-angle weave to finish the end wall of the bracelet.

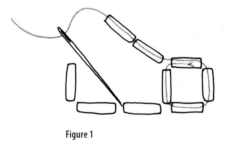

Figure 1

5 Continue down the strip, making interior walls down the three horizontal rows of bugles. Work right-angle weave across the top of the walls to finish the now three-dimensional rows (Figure 2).

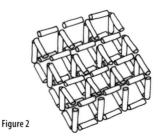

Figure 2

6 Sew one half of the clasp firmly to the horizontal bugles at one end of the bracelet. Repeat at the other end.

7 Begin a new thread in the corner of an intersection at the bottom of the bracelet. Pass through a bugle, string a charlotte or Delica, and pass through the adjoining bugle. This will make the weaves square and give them extra strength. Continue across the bottom of the bracelet, adding charlottes or Delicas to each intersection. Be sure to pull the thread gently, but keep a firm tension to snap the beads into position. Repeat for the top of the bracelet.

8 Begin a new doubled thread, at an intersection at the top of the bracelet. String 1 charlotte, 1 crystal, and 1 charlotte. Pass through the diagonal intersection bead. Repeat, adding crystals or pearls at a diagonal across the top and sides of the bracelet (Figure 3). Don't embellish the bottom of the bracelet that touches the wrist.

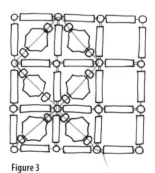

Figure 3

Pearls and Twists

Lilli Brennan

This bracelet is a clever working of wire and pearls. It encircles your wrist like a golden guard!

Materials

44 white 4mm glass pearls

2 gold-filled or brass nontarnish jump rings

6mm gold magnetic clasp

6' (180 cm) of 22-gauge gold-filled or brass nontarnish wire

2' (60 cm) of 20-gauge gold-filled or brass nontarnish wire

Tools

Table

Cotton pads

Hand drill

Cup hook bit

Cotton pads

Wire cutters

Nylon-jaw pliers

WigJig Cyclops

Techniques

Wirework, stringing

See pages 119–125 for how-tos

1 Fold the 22-gauge wire in half and wrap it around a table leg. Protect the leg with cotton pads. Place the cup hook in the drill and secure the wire to the cup hook. While holding the wire tight, slowly turn the drill handle (Figure 1). Twist the wire on the drill until you get a consistent, tight twist that resembles a rope. Clip the wire from the hook and table leg. If necessary, gently straighten the wire with nylon-jaw pliers.

Figure 1

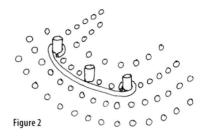

Figure 2

Figure 3

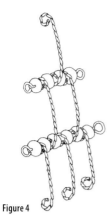

Figure 4

2 Make a simple loop on one end of the twisted wire and place it on the upper left peg of the jig (Figure 2). Bring the wire tail to the far right peg and form a loop around that peg to make a link. Remove the link from the jig and clip the wire tail (Figure 3). Repeat to form 20 links in all.

3 Make a simple loop on one end of a 3" (7.5 cm) piece of 20-gauge wire. String pearls and links in the pattern shown (Figure 4) to form the center section of the bracelet. Make a simple loop to secure the stringing sequence, and trim the wire. Repeat, following Figure 5 to form the entire bracelet. Note that for the end link you add only 4 pearls and 1 link.

4 Use a jump ring to attach one half of the clasp to the single link at one end of the bracelet. Repeat for the other side.

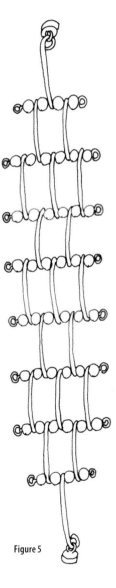

Figure 5

Slither Chain

Jane Tyson

This versatile bracelet is a natural for any attire. Alternating matte and shiny beads of the same color makes a very effective look.

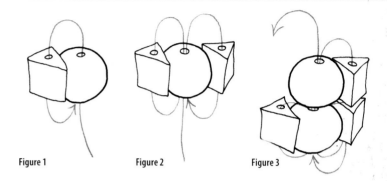

Figure 1   Figure 2   Figure 3

Materials

3–4 g size 11° triangle beads

6 g size 8° seed beads in two colors

Size B Nymo beading thread in color to match beads

Small clasp

1.4mm gimp (French wire) to match clasp

Beeswax or Thread Heaven

Tools

Size 10 or 12 beading needle

Scissors

Technique

Ladder stitch (modified)

See pages 119–125 for how-to

1 Using 3' (90 cm) of conditioned thread, string 1 size 8° and 1 triangle, leaving a 15" (37.5 cm) tail. Pass through the size 8° again so the triangle sits next to the size 8° (Figure 1).

2 String 1 triangle and pass up through the size 8°. You should now have 1 size 8° with 1 triangle on either side (Figure 2).

3 String 1 size 8° and 1 triangle bead. Pass down through the right-hand triangle and up through the 2 center size 8°s (Figure 3). String 1 triangle and pass down through the left-hand triangle and up through the 2 center size 8°s.

4 Repeat Step 3 until you reach the desired length minus the width of the clasp.

5 String 7⁄16" (1 cm) of gimp and weave the gimp through the loop on one half of the clasp. Pass back into the beadwork and through the gimp again to reinforce. Secure the thread and trim.

6 Repeat Step 5 at the other end of the bracelet to attach the other half of the clasp.

Tips

- Cull your beads for this project. Many triangle beads are off shape. Try to use only the triangles with straight ends. Make sure they are about the same height vertically as the seed beads. If anything, the triangles should be a little shorter than the seed beads.
- Watch your tension. Do not pull your beads too close together.
- Check that you have passed through the center beads without piercing the thread within. Once pierced, the thread is almost impossible to work through.

Netted Garden

Margo C. Field

Making this pretty bracelet is just the thing to bring you down to earth. After you create the netted base, you'll decorate the bracelet with seed and accent beads, or what Margo likes to call "planting the garden."

Materials

Size 11° seed beads in two colors, A and B

Size 11° seed beads in five colors for the garden

Assortment of 3mm and 4mm accent beads (fire-polished beads, druks, squares, pearls)

Button with shank

Size B Nymo beading thread in color to match beads

Beeswax

Tools

Size 12 beading or sharp needle

Scissors

Techniques

Tension bead, netting, fringe, button-and-loop clasp

See pages 119–125 for how-to

1 Use 6' (180 cm) of waxed thread and make a tension bead, leaving a 2' (60 cm) tail. String 22A and pass back through the seventeenth bead strung.

2 String 3A, skip the next 3A strung in Step 1, and pass back through the next A. Continue working netting across, stringing 3A and skipping 3A (Figure 1). Tighten so the work is snug.

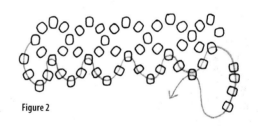
Figure 1

3 String 4A and pass through the second bead of the last 3-bead group added in Step 2. *String 3A and pass through the second bead of the next 3-bead group. Repeat from * across (Figure 2). *Note:* The last stitch passes back through the twenty-first strung in Step 1.

Figure 2

4 Repeat Step 3 for the desired length, minus the length of the clasp. Secure the thread and trim.

5 Begin a new 6' (180 cm) length of thread at the end of the bracelet base and exit from the first shared bead on the first row (where you made your first net). String 3B. Pass through the first shared bead on the second row, making sure to pass through in the same direction so your beads create a slant (Figure 3). Repeat down the entire length of

Figure 3

the base. Weave through the beads and embellish the other side of the base in the same way.

6 Exit from a shared bead at one corner of the base and begin to "plant the garden." String 3B and pass through the next shared bead of that row. *Use garden-colored size 11°s to make 1 leaf on each side of the shared bead. To make a leaf, string 6 size 11°s, pass back through the fifth bead just strung, string 3 size 11°s, and pass back through the first bead just strung (Figure 4). Pass through the base bead last exited and repeat to make another leaf. Tie a knot between beads on the base to secure the leaves. String 3 vine-colored beads, weave to the next shared bead, and repeat from *.

Figure 4

Variations

- Make the vine curvy by passing through a common bead of an adjoining row. You may have to add more than 3 beads to cover the space.
- Instead of making leaves, make a short fringe using size 11°s and an accent bead.
- End the vine at any point and start it somewhere else.
- Put a little leaf in an empty space all by itself.

7 Exiting from a center bead at the end of the bracelet, make a basic button-and-loop clasp.

Fences and Flowers

Jeri Herrera

This seemingly complicated pattern is a snap! Just follow the instructions and illustrations, and use the crystal placement as your guide.

Materials

Size 11° Japanese seed beads

4mm Swarovski crystal bicones

3-loop clasp

Size D Nymo beading thread

Tools

Size 12 beading or sharp needle

Scissors

Technique

Right-angle weave

See pages 119–125 for how-to

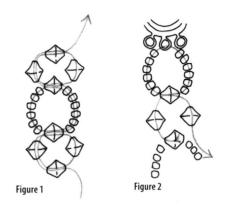

Figure 1   Figure 2

1 Use 6' (180 cm) of thread to string 4 crystals, leaving a 4" tail (10 cm). Tie a knot to make a circle. Pass through the crystals again to reinforce.

2 String 6 seed beads, 1 crystal, and 6 seed beads. Pass through the third crystal strung in Step 1. Pass through the first 6 seed beads and the crystal strung in this step.

3 String 3 crystals and pass through the single crystal strung in the previous step and the first 2 just strung (Figure 1).

4 Repeat Steps 2 and 3 until the bracelet is the desired length minus the length of the clasp.

5 String 6 seed beads, pass through the center clasp loop, and string 6 seed beads. Pass through the beads just added several times to reinforce. Weave through the beads to exit from the right-hand crystal as shown in Figure 2.

6 String 3 seed beads, 1 crystal, 6 seed beads, 1 crystal, and 3 seed beads. Pass through the crystal you last exited in Step 5. Pass through the first 3 seed beads, 1 crystal, 6 seed beads, and 1 crystal just strung.

7 String 5 seed beads and pass through the right-hand clasp loop. Pass back through the seed beads just strung. Weave through the loop of beads again to reinforce. Exit from the crystal farthest from the clasp.

8 String 3 crystals and pass through the crystal you last exited (Figure 3). Exit from the second crystal of the 3 just added. String 3 seed beads and pass through the right-hand crystal as shown in Figure 4.

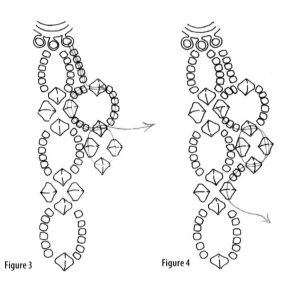

Figure 3   Figure 4

9 String 3 seed beads, 1 crystal, and 6 seed beads. Pass through the closest crystal from the loop created in Step 7. Pass through the first 3 seed beads just added, the adjacent crystal from the original row (Steps 2 and 3), the next 3 seed beads and 1 crystal just added. String 6 seed beads, 1 crystal, and 3 seed beads. Pass through the adjacent crystal from the original row. Repeat Steps 8 and 9 down the entire length of the bracelet.

10 When you reach the end, complete the last loop and weave through the very first crystal of the bracelet. String 6 seed beads and pass through the middle loop of the other half of the clasp. String 6 more seed beads. Weave through the loop of beads again to reinforce.

11 Pass back through the last crystal in the last loop of the second row. String 5 seed beads and pass through the next loop in the clasp. Pass back through the 5 seed beads and around the loop. Weave through the beads again to reinforce and exit from the first outside crystal on the left-hand side of the bracelet.

12 String 3 seed beads, 1 crystal, 6 seed beads, 1 crystal, and 3 seed beads. Pass through the crystal on the original row and the beads and last crystal just added (Figure 5).

Figure 5

13 String 5 seed beads. Pass through the third loop in the clasp. Weave through the beads again to reinforce. Work down the other side of the bracelet as you did for the first side. When you reach the end, string 5 seed beads, pass through the last open clasp loop and back through the seed beads just strung. Weave through the beads again to reinforce. Secure the thread and trim.

Three-Step Bracelet

Margo C. Field

Make this bracelet by weaving a band of flat peyote stitch and then embellishing it with appliqué and a picot edging. The result is a delicate but sophisticated-looking chain.

Materials

Size 15° seed beads

Size 11° seed beads

Delica beads

Button for clasp

Size B Nymo or Silamide beading thread

Beeswax

Tools

Size 10 and 12 beading needles

Scissors

Techniques

Peyote stitch, picot edging, button-and-loop clasp

See pages 119–125 for how-tos

1 Use 6' (180 cm) of waxed thread to string 2 Delicas, leaving a 2' (60 cm) tail. Pass through the first bead just strung.

2 String 3 Delicas. Pass through the second bead just strung.

3 Reinforce the beads by passing back through the fifth, third, second, and first beads to make the beads look like a capital "I" (Figure 1).

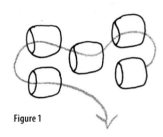

Figure 1

4 String 1 size 11° and pass through the fourth and fifth beads.

5 String 1 Delica and pass through the second bead.

6 String 1 Delica and pass through the bead strung in the previous step and the edge bead on the diagonal (Figure 2).

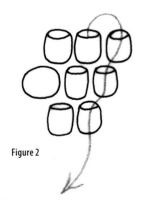

Figure 2

7 String 1 Delica and pass through the center bead and the edge bead on the diagonal (Figure 3).

Figure 3

8 Pass through the next edge bead. String 1 Delica and pass through the edge bead on the other side.

9 Repeat Steps 6–8 until you reach the desired length minus the length of the clasp. The last bead added should be a size 11°, as in Step 4.

10 Exit from the center end size 11° and string 3 size 15°s. Skip the next center bead and pass through the second center bead in the same direction so that the thread exits from the same side of the bead as it did before. This will make the 3 beads lie diagonally. Continue to the other end. *Note:* You will be using all the odd-count center beads and will end up in the size 11° at the end.

11 Weave through the beads to exit from the first edge bead of the 3-bead peyote strip. String 3 size 15°s. Pass under the first exposed thread loop at the edge and pass back through the third bead just strung. String 2 size 15°s. Pass under the next exposed thread loop and pass back through the second bead just strung. Repeat to the end to create an edging (Figure 4).

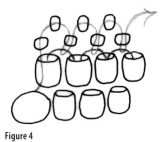

Figure 4

12 Repeat Step 11 for the other side of the bracelet.

13 Use the tail thread to attach a basic button-and-loop clasp.

Wagon Wheels

Sharon Bateman

These wheels roll across your wrist like wagons on the trail. By altering the type and color of beads used for the spokes, you've got a whole different look.

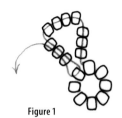

Figure 1

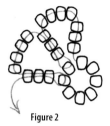

Figure 2

Materials

Size 11° seed beads in an assortment of colors

Button for clasp

Beading thread in color to match the beads

White glue

Tools

Size 12 needle

Scissors

Techniques

Square stitch, button-and-loop clasp

See pages 119–125 for how-tos

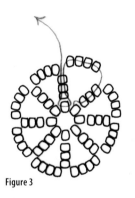

Figure 3

Whole Wheel

Round 1: Use 3' (90 cm) of thread to string 8 beads, leaving a 6" (15 cm) tail. Tie a knot to form a foundation circle. Trim the tail and secure the end with glue. String 10 beads. Pass through the next bead of the foundation circle and up through the last 3 beads of the 10 just added (Figure 1).

String 7 beads. Pass through the next bead of the foundation circle and up through the last 3 beads of the 7 just added (Figure 2). Repeat around the circle five times until you have 8 spokes in all.

String 4 beads. Pass down through the first 3-bead spoke of the round. Pass through the first bead of the circle and back up through the first spoke (Figure 3).

Round 2: String 2 beads. Pass through the first 2 beads of the closest spoke and back through the 2 beads just added to make a square stitch. String 3 beads. Pass through the next 2 beads of the last round and back through the last 2 beads of the 3 just added (Figure 4).

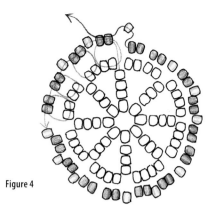

Figure 4

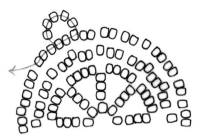

Figure 5

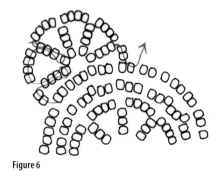

Figure 6

String 3 beads. Pass back through the next 2 beads of the last round and through the last 2 beads of the 3 just added. String 2 beads and pass back through the next 2 beads of the last round and the 2 just added. Repeat around the circle. String 1 bead and pass through the first 2 beads added in this round.

Round 3: String 2 beads. Square-stitch these 2 beads onto the next 2 beads of the previous round. String 3 beads. Pass through the next 2 beads of the last round and back through the last 2 of the 3 just added. Repeat all around until you have only 4 beads left on the last round. Square-stitch 2 beads to the 2 beads below on the previous round twice. String 1 bead and pass through the first set of 2 beads in this round to close it.

Half Wheels
Make 9 consecutive half-wheels, working each new wheel directly on the previous wheel.

Round 1: String 5 beads. Pass into the last wheel 3 beads away from where the thread exited and then through 6 beads to the left (Figure 5).

Round 2: String 5 beads and pass through the first bead of Round 1 and back up through the last 3 beads just added. Pull tight.

String 7 beads. Pass through the next bead of Round 1 and back up through the last 3 beads just added (Figure 6). Pull tight. Repeat three more times to make 5 spokes in all. String 2 beads. Pass through the fourth bead from the end of Round 1.

Round 3: String 3 beads. Square-stitch the last 2 beads added onto the first 2 beads of the last round. Repeat around to the opposite side. Exit from the second bead up from Round 1 on the last wheel.

Round 4: String 3 beads. Square-stitch the last 2 of the 3 beads just added onto the first 2 beads of the last round. Stitch 2 beads onto the 2 beads below on the previous round for 2 more sets. Repeat to the opposite side. String 1 bead. Pass through the second bead on the last wheel, up from Round 3. Pass through 20 beads to the top of the wheel.

Clasp
Use the working and tail threads to attach a basic button-and-loop clasp.

Serendipity Bangles

Theresa Grout

Make these fun bangles as simple or as fringed as you like. Add fringe legs, fringe loops, or fringe ruffles for a variety of effects.

Materials

Assortment of size 14° or 11° seed beads

Size 6° seed beads

Size 4° pony beads

64–96 Czech pressed-glass 8mm or larger beads

12–24mm clasp bead

Beading thread in color to match beads

Tools

Size 10 beading or Big Eye needle

Scissors

Techniques

Peyote stitch, fringe, button-and-loop clasp

See pages 119–125 for how-tos

1 Use a size 6° and 6' (180 cm) of thread to create a tension bead, leaving an 8" (20 cm) tail. String 1 size 4° and 1 size 6°. Repeat until you have a total of 64 beads.

2 Work five rows of peyote stitch using size 6°s (incorporate the tension bead into your work). Work one row using size 4°s. Your bracelet should have a total of eight rows.

3 Fold the first and last rows together and zip the edges to make a tube. Weave through the beads to exit from the end of the tube.

4 Use 3 size 6°s, the clasp bead, and 1 size 6° to make the button portion of the button-and-loop clasp. Weave through the beads several times to reinforce. Secure the thread and trim. Use size 6°s and the tail thread to make the loop portion of the clasp. Weave through the beads several times to reinforce. Secure the thread and trim.

5 Begin a new thread that exits from the end size 4° along the tube's seam. String 6 to 10 small seed beads, 1 pressed-glass bead, and 1 small seed bead. Skipping the last bead strung, pass back through all but the first 2 beads strung. String 2 small seed beads and pass through the next size 4° along the seam (Figure 1). Continue adding fringe legs down the seam until you reach the end. For a very full fringe, work back across the tube, adding fringe legs between each size 6° along the seam.

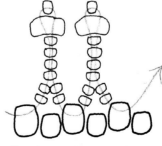

Figure 1

Flower Garden

Ellen Sadler

This lovely bracelet brings springtime flowers year-round! Once you learn how to construct one of the pretty flowers, you'll be able to create new variations, making your own unique garden.

Materials

Size 11° seed beads for the flower bodies
Size 8° and 11° green seed beads for the base
Size 8° seed and drop beads for the flower centers
Beading thread in color to match beads

Tools

Size 12 beading or sharp needle
Scissors

Techniques

Right-angle weave, brick stitch, ladder stitch, peyote stitch
See pages 119–125 for how-tos

1 Use 6' (180 cm) of thread to string 1 green size 11°, 1 green size 8°, and 1 green size 11° four times. Tie a knot to form a circle and pass through the first 3 beads strung. This is your first right-angle weave unit, with 1 size 11°, 1 size 8°, and 1 size 11° making up each side. Continue working right-angle weave until you have a strip five units wide by twenty-four rows long. Add more rows as necessary for length. Secure the thread and trim close to the work. Set the band aside.

2 Use 3' (90 cm) of thread and green size 11°s to make a brick-stitched square 6 beads wide by six rows long. Tightly zip the side edges together to create a tube. Secure the thread and trim. Repeat to make a second tube. Set the tubes aside.

3 Use 3' (90 cm) of thread and green size 11°s to make a strip of ladder stitch 6 beads long. Work brick stitch off the top of the ladder, decreasing to a point. Weave through the triangle to the bottom of the ladder-stitched strip and work brick stitch, decreasing to a point so you end up with a leaf shape (Figure 1). Repeat to make a second leaf. Sew the face of one of the leaves to the side of one of the tubes. Repeat for the remaining leaf and tube. Set all aside.

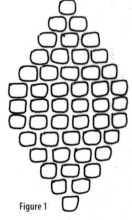

Figure 1

4 Begin a new thread at one end of the band. Reinforce the end by adding 1 size 11° between each size 11° (Figure 2).

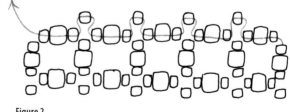

Figure 2

Figure 3

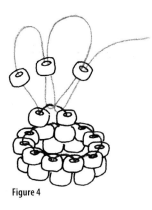

Figure 4

5 Exit from a 3-bead group closest to one side of the band. String 4 size 11's. Weave through beads down the side of one of the tubes. String 4 size 11's. Pass through the 3-bead group you last exited. Pass through all again to reinforce. Weave through the beads along the end of the band to exit from the 3-bead group at the opposite corner. Repeat to attach the second clasp (Figure 3).

6 Reinforce the other end of the band as you did in Step 4. Exit from a corner bead and string 21 size 11's or enough to fit around the leaf at the other end of the band. Skip two 3-bead groups at the end of the band and pass through the fourth 3-bead group. Make a second loop and pass back through the last size 11° of this row of the band. Weave through all the beads again to reinforce. Set the bracelet base aside.

7 Use 3' (90 cm) of thread and the flower body beads to work an even-count strip of ladder stitch 12 or fewer beads wide; leave a 6" (15 cm) tail. Weave the first and last beads together to make a circle. Work brick stitch off the ladder-stitched strip for 1 or 2 rounds to create your flower base. The exposed thread between each bead at the top of the tube will be called "bridges."

8 *Note:* In the bracelet shown, every flower is worked differently. These instructions are for the basic techniques, not for each flower. Divide the number of bridges by the number of desired petals. This will help you calculate how many beads to work on each bridge in the first row of each petal. For example, if you have twelve bridges and want four petals, you will work the first row over three bridges. Use brick stitch to work each petal, increasing or decreasing as needed (Figure 4). Once the point is worked, weave down through the rows to the flower base and begin the next petal.

You can work each flower differently by:
• Changing the number of beads in the flower base. This will change the number of petals you can add, or the width of the base row of each petal.
• Altering the height of the flower base by adding more layers.
• Varying the width, length, and points of the petals to produce different effects. You can even alternate variations of the petals on the same flower.
• Changing the color(s) and the pattern in which you use the colors can alter the effect of the flower.

9 Repeat Steps 7–8 until you have twenty-seven flowers in all. Set all aside.

10 Use the flowers' tails to sew them randomly to the bracelet base. Start at one corner of the bracelet and work your way across. Secure each flower by passing through one of the beads on the bracelet base and then passing back up through the flower base. Add seed or drop beads to the centers to finish each flower. Alternate sewing through the bracelet base and the flower base until each flower is secure. Secure the thread and trim.

Peekaboo Bracelet

Jane Tyson

A combination of square and odd-count peyote stitches, this bracelet resembles chain link.

Materials

10 g large Delica beads

10 g size 8° hex beads

12mm fold-over clasp with 7 holes

Nymo beading thread in color to match beads

Tools

Size 12 beading or sharp needle

Scissors

Techniques

Tension bead, square stitch, peyote stitch

See pages 119–125 for how-tos

1 Use 3' (90 cm) of thread to string a tension bead, leaving a 12" (30 cm) tail. String 1 Delica, 1 hex, 1 Delica, 1 hex, 1 Delica, 1 hex, and 2 Delicas.

2 Begin a row of peyote stitch by passing back through the last hex strung. String 1 Delica and pass through the next hex. String 1 Delica and pass through the next hex. String 1 Delica and pass through the first Delica strung, exiting your thread toward the center of the beadwork (Figure 1).

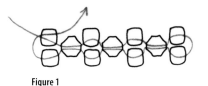

Figure 1

3 Use hex beads to work peyote stitch across the row. When finished, pass through the adjacent Delica, exiting toward the center of the beadwork (Figure 2).

Figure 2

Variations on the Peekaboo bracelet: Gold and green bracelets by Donna Zaidenburg

4 *String 1 Delica and square-stitch it to the Delica you last exited. Pass through 1 hex and 1 Delica. Repeat from * three times so you have four columns with three Delicas in each. Pass through the last Delica added, exiting toward the center of the beadwork (Figure 3).

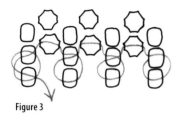

Figure 3

5 Use hex beads to work peyote stitch between each Delica added in the last step to add a total of 3 hex beads (Figure 4).

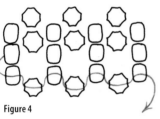

Figure 4

6 Use Delicas to work peyote stitch between each hex added in the last step. Use square stitch to add the last Delica, exiting away from the center of the beadwork (Figure 5).

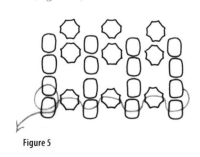

Figure 5

7 String 1 Delica and work square stitch to attach it to the Delica you last exited. String 1 hex and 1 Delica and work square stitch to attach the Delica to the next Delica of the previous row. Repeat to the end of the row (Figure 6).

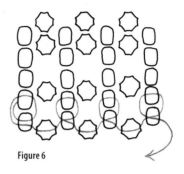

Figure 6

8 Repeat Steps 6 and 7 until you reach the desired length, minus the width of the clasp. End with a row that looks like Figure 5. Use the working thread to sew the last row of the bracelet to one half of the clasp. Remove the tension bead and use the tail to sew the first row to the other half of the clasp.

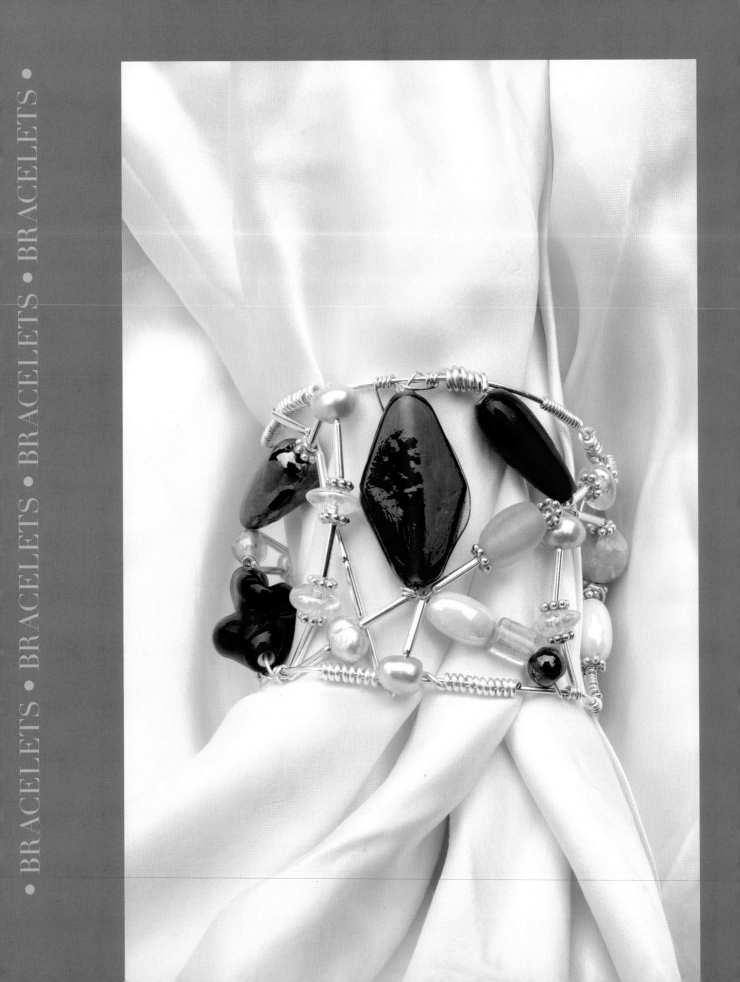

Cuffed

Jean Campbell

Create this fanciful wire cuff in an evening. Let the beads be your design guide.

Materials

4' (120 cm) of 14-gauge silver wire

6' (180 cm) of 18-gauge silver wire

Assorted beads including pressed glass, pearls, and liquid silver

8½" (21.3 cm) wide piece of paper

Tools

Scissors

Wire cutter

Needle-nose pliers

Technique

Wirework

See pages 119–125 for how-to

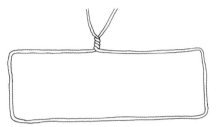

Figure 1

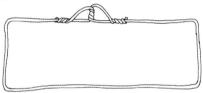

Figure 2

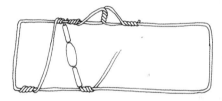

Figure 3

1 Cut a strip of paper as wide and as long as you'd like the final bracelet to be. The bracelet shown is 2" (5 cm) wide and 7" long.

2 Beginning at the upper left corner of the paper's perimeter, lay the 14-gauge wire across the length of the paper. When you reach the first corner, use the needle-nose pliers to bend a 90-degree angle. Continue around the outside of the paper, making bends at the corners. When you finish the last corner, leave enough wire to run across the length of the rectangle and cut the wire.

3 Take the wires that lie across the top of the rectangle and make two twists at the center (Figure 1). Bend them back and coil them on themselves (Figure 2).

4 Cut an 8" (20 cm) length of 18-gauge wire and coil the end around the 14-gauge wire at one corner. Slide on enough beads to reach the other edge of the wire rectangle. Attach the beads by coiling the 18-gauge wire around the 14-gauge wire. Continue adding beads and weaving back and forth on the rectangle (Figure 3). Also weave from one 18-gauge length to another to achieve a webbed effect.

If you find you need more wire for weaving, simply end the old one by coiling it off and trimming it close to the wire. Start a new one by repeating Step 4.

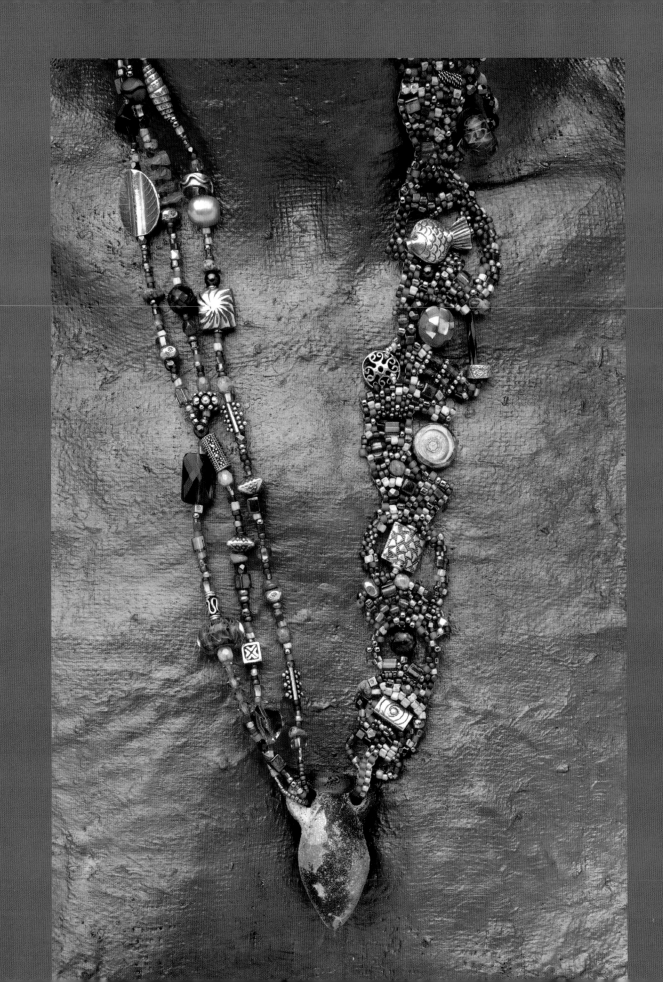

Vesselage

Anna Karena

Inspired by the focal vessel made by Minneapolis lampworker Annemarie Herrlich, this free-form necklace evolved on its own. When making yours, do away with preplanning and let the beads speak to you.

Materials

Size 6°, 8°, 11°, and 15° seed beads in a palette of colors to
    match the vessel
Pearl, semiprecious stone, glass, and silver beads
Lampworked vessel
6 crimp tubes
2-loop clasp
Size B beading thread
.014 beading wire

Tools

Size 12 beading or sharp needles
Scissors
Measuring tape
Wire cutters

Techniques

Peyote stitch, stringing
See pages 119–125 for how-tos

1 Begin by working a 2-bead-wide peyote strip (Figure 1). Work the strap long enough to fit around the vessel handle. Wrap the strip around the handle and zip the edges together.

2 Continue working peyote stitch off of the strip, increasing your stitches to begin the free-form

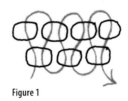

Figure 1

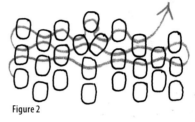

Figure 2

work. Anything is fair game when you're working free-form beadwork. You can make increases by adding extra beads mid-row (Figure 2), or you can gently change the shape and feeling of your beadwork by changing the shape and size of beads used.

Another component in free-form beadwork is the incorporation of larger beads. Here are two ways to do it.

For a horizontal hole, string a few beads off your peyote-stitched row. String the larger bead and a few beads. Weave through the beads on the last row and exit from the beads strung before the larger bead (Figure 3). Work new rows of peyote stitch off these beads. When you reach the larger bead, string enough beads to pass over the top of the larger bead. Work peyote stitch off the beads strung on the other side of the larger bead. Continue working back and forth above the bead (Figure 4).

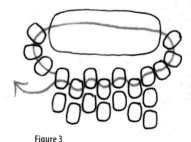

Figure 3

Figure 4

For a vertical hole, decide where you'd like your bead to go and string a seed bead, the larger bead, and a seed bead. Pass back through the larger bead and the seed bead, then peyote stitch to the end of the row.

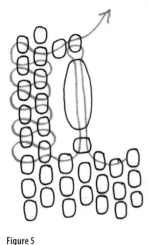

*Work a thin strip of peyote stitch tall enough to reach the seed bead at the top of the larger bead. String enough beads to reach the top of the larger bead. Pass back through the larger bead and to the other side of the peyote row. Repeat from * for the other side of the row. Continue working peyote stitch as usual all across the row (Figure 5).

Figure 5

3 Work in free-form peyote stitch until you reach half the desired necklace length. *Note:* The end of this section will hang in the middle of the back of your neck and cleanly attach to the clasp—make adjustments to width accordingly.

At the end of the strap, use size 15°s to work two short strips of 2-bead-wide peyote stitch. These will help connect the free-form strap to the clasp. Make the strips long enough to reach through and wrap around the loops on one half of the clasp; pass each strip through the loops and sew back into the beadwork

to make a firm connection. Weave through the strips again to reinforce. Secure the thread and trim close to the work.

4 Measure the length of the first side of your necklace. Add 3" (7.5 cm) and cut that measurement of wire. Attach the wire to one of the loops on the other half of the clasp using a crimp tube.

5 String an assortment of beads. Pay attention to the placement of the larger beads on the other side of the necklace, making sure you don't string them directly across from their counterparts on the other side. Create a few surprises by making sure that each side has a few beads the other side does not.

6 When you reach about 1½" (3.8 cm) from the end, string 1 crimp tube and 1¼" (3.1 cm) of seed beads. Pass through the other arm of the vessel and back through the tube. Snug the beads and crimp. Trim the tail close to the work.

7 Repeat Steps 4–6 twice so you end up with three strung strands in all.

Pearl Net Choker

Linda Richmond

Make this versatile choker by working rounds of netting. Change the number and size of the pearls, seed beads, and stitches, and you'll have a completely different look!

Materials

Size 15° seed beads in color to match pearls

Delica beads in color to match pearls

Six 16" strands of 3.5–4mm small button or round pearls

2 sterling silver 8–12mm bead caps

Sterling silver hook-and-eye clasp

Size O Nymo beading thread in color to match beads

Glue or nail polish

Beeswax

Tools

Size 15 beading needles

Scissors

Measuring tape

Technique

Netting

See pages 119–125 for how-to

---

thread to pull it through beads; don't use your needle to pull your thread or the eye will break.

Round 2: String 1 Delica, 1 size 15°, 1 Delica, 1 pearl, 1 Delica, 1 size 15°, and 1 Delica. Pass through the second pearl of the first round (Figure 1). Repeat this pattern for the rest of this round, passing through every other pearl. After passing through the last pearl of the first round, step up to the next round by passing through the Delica, size 15°, Delica, and pearl of this round.

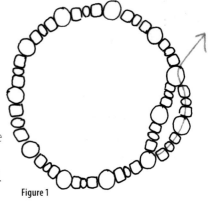

Figure 1

1 Work rounds of netting.

Round 1: Use 3' (90 cm) of doubled, waxed thread to string 1 pearl, 1 Delica, 1 size 15°, and 1 Delica twelve times, leaving a 6" (15 cm) tail. Tie a knot to form a circle. Step up to the next round by passing through the next Delica, size 15°, Delica, and pearl. *Note:* Size 15 beading needles are very fragile, so always hold your

Round 3: String 1 Delica, 1 size 15°, 1 Delica, 1 pearl, 1 Delica, 1 size 15°, and 1 Delica. Pass through the next pearl (you no longer skip a pearl). Repeat around and make the step up.

Repeat Round 3 until you've used all the pearls.

2 Measure the length you'd like your choker to be and subtract the length of the pearl netting portion you just completed. Following the instructions below will give you 1⅝" (4.1 cm) of netting for each side, plus another 1" (2.5 cm) for the caps and hook and eye. By adjusting your numbers a bit, you can decide whether you should complete the number of rounds given in the steps below or work more or fewer rounds in each step to achieve your desired length.

Round 1: String 3 Delicas, 1 size 15°, and 3 Delicas. Pass through the next pearl of the previous round. Repeat this step around. Step up by passing through 3 Delicas and 1 size 15°.

Round 2: String 3 Delicas, 1 size 15°, and 3 Delicas. Pass through the next size 15° of the previous round. Repeat around and make the step up.

Round 3: Repeat Round 2.

Rounds 4–12: String 2 Delicas, 1 size 15°, and 2 Delicas. Pass through the next size 15° of the previous round. Make the step up.

Rounds 13–18: String 1 Delica, 1 size 15°, and 1 Delica. Pass through the next size 15° of the previous round. Make the step up (Figure 2).

3 String 1 bead cap and one half of the clasp. Pass back through the bead cap. Snug the cap down over the beadwork and pull the thread tight.

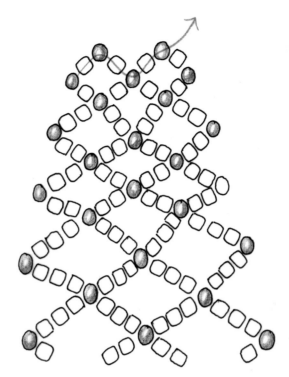

Figure 2

4 Pass through the next size 15° in the last round of the beadwork, up through the cap and clasp, and back through the cap. Keep the cap even over the beadwork as you snug the thread evenly and tightly. Continue to reinforce the cap by passing through the size 15°s on the last round of the beadwork, up through the cap and clasp, and back through the cap. Secure the thread and seal knots with glue or nail polish. Trim the tail and working thread close to the work.

5 Repeat Steps 2–4 to complete the other side of the choker.

Victorian Necklace

Lisa Norris

Create this elegant necklace by adding a swirl of picots and loops to peyote-stitched strips.

Materials

Size 11° gold Delica beads

Size 11° amethyst Delica beads

12 topaz AB 5mm Swarovski crystal bicones

10–20mm topaz crystal and brass ornament

French bullion or gimp

Clasp

Size B Nymo beading thread

Tools

Size 12 beading or sharp needle

Scissors

Techniques

Tension bead, peyote stitch, ladder stitch, picots

See pages 119–125 for how-tos

1 Use 6' (180 cm) of thread and 1 gold Delica to string a tension bead, leaving an 8" (20 cm) tail. String 2 gold Delicas and pass back through the tension bead. Adjust the beads just strung so the second bead sits on top of the first one. String 1 gold Delica and pass back through the last bead just strung (Figure 1). Repeat to make a strip 15–16" (37.5–40 cm) long.

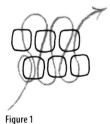

Figure 1

2 String ⅜" (.9 cm) of French bullion and one half of the clasp. Pass back through the last bead added to make a loop. Weave through all again to reinforce. Use the tail thread to repeat on the other end of the strip.

3 Repeat Step 1 to make a 2-bead-wide-by-8–9" (20–22.5 cm) long strip of peyote stitch. Work a 5–6 bead strip of ladder stitch at each end of the peyote-stitched strip. Each end should have its ladder-stitched portion on the same side (top).

4 Lay the longer strip in a circle. Place the center of the shorter strip 1" (2.5 cm) below the center of the longer one. Curve the shorter strip up to meet the longer one. Sew the last 3 beads of the ladder-stitched strips to the longer strip.

5 Work a series of amethyst Delica picots and loops from the point of attachment back to the clasp (Figure 2). Make a picot by stringing 4 beads and passing back through the first bead just strung. Pass through the bead on the peyote-stitched strip next to the bead you exited to start the picot. Pass through the bead that sits below/between the two top beads so your needle travels in a triangle shape.

Make a loop by stringing 8 beads, skipping 3 beads on the peyote-stitched strip, and passing through the fourth bead. When you pass

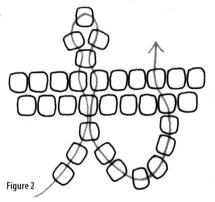

Figure 2

up through the strip, make sure your needle is angled so that when the next picot is made, the bottom bead of the picot will be directly above the top bead of the loop.

Repeat for the other side of the necklace.

6 Begin a new thread and exit from the third bead down the strip from the first picot made in Step 5. Use amethyst Delicas to make a series of picots and loops along the top strip, but gradually increase the distance between loops. Use 6 Delicas for loops 1–4 and skip 3 beads on the strip between each loop. Use 4 Delicas, 1 crystal, and 4 Delicas for loops 5–7 and skip 4 beads on the strip. Use 5 Delicas, 1 crystal, and 5 Delicas for loops 8 and 9 and skip 5 beads on

the strip. For the tenth loop, use 16 Delicas and skip 6 beads on the strip.

Work in reverse order to the other side of the necklace.

7 Weave the thread to the bottom strip. Exit from the third peyote-stitched bead down from the ladder-stitched portion of the strip. Make a picot and pass through the strip into the center of the necklace. String 1 amethyst Delica and pass through the center two beads of the opposing loop. String 2 amethyst Delicas, skip 3 beads on the strip, and pass through the bottom strip. Make a picot on the opposite side. String 2 amethyst Delicas and pass through the center two beads of the opposing loops. String 2 amethyst Delicas, skip 3 beads on the strip, and pass through the bottom strip and make a picot.

Continue to work picots and loops using all amethyst Delicas in the following bead counts. Use 3 for Loop 3, passing through the center 2 beads of the opposing loop and skipping 4 beads on the peyote strip. Use 3 for Loop 4, passing through the crystal of the opposing loop and skipping 4 beads on the peyote strip. Use 4 for Loop 5, passing through the crystal and skipping 5 beads on the peyote strip. Use 5 for Loop 6, passing through the crystal and skipping 5 beads. Use 6 for Loop 7, skipping 5 beads on the peyote strip. Use 7 for Loop 8, skipping 6 beads. Use 8 for Loop 9, skipping 6 beads. For Loop 10, string 7 Delicas and pass through the middle 2 beads of the opposing loop. String 7 and skip 7 beads on the peyote strip.

Work the loops in reverse order to the other side of the necklace.

8 Sew the crystal ornament to the center loop. Weave in all working and tail threads and trim close to the work.

Topaz Beauty

Pat Mayer

Sparkly Wheel designed by Nikia Angel

Combine simple peyote-stitched tubes, crystals, and a swirling Sparkly Wheel to make this stunning topaz necklace.

Materials

Size 11° Japanese seed beads or Delica beads

27 Swarovski crystal 4mm bicones

1 Swarovski crysal 4mm round

17 Swarovski crystal 6mm or 8mm AB rounds

32 Swarovski crystal-inlaid 5mm or 6mm flat rondelles

1 large Swarovski crystal vertically drilled drop

2 crimp tubes

Clasp

Size B Nymo beading thread in color to match beads

32" (80 cm) of size .019 Soft Flex beading wire or 20 lb Power Pro
    beading thread

Beeswax or thread conditioner

Tools

Size 11 or 12 beading needle

Crimping pliers

Wire cutters

Scissors

Techniques

Tension bead, peyote stitch, netting, stringing

See pages 119–125 for how-tos

Note: Instructions are for a 16" necklace. For each extra inch of neck-
    lace length, add 1 crystal, 1 peyote-stitched tube, and 2 rondelles.

Sparkly Wheel

1 Use 2½' (75 cm) of doubled, waxed thread to string a tension bead, leaving an 8" (20 cm) tail. String one 4mm bicone and 3 size 11's nine times. Remove the tension bead. Tie a knot to form a circle. Exit from the second size 11° strung.

2 Working with a tight tension, string 5 size 11's and pass through the center bead of the next set of size 11's. Repeat around the circle (Figure 1). Weave through the beads to exit from the center bead of the first set of size 11's added in this step.

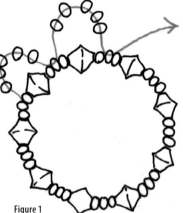

Figure 1

3 String one 4mm bicone and pass through the center bead of the next set of size 11°s (Figure 2). Repeat around the circle, to add a total of 9 crystals. As you work, gently push the beads toward the inside of the circle created in Step 2. Weave through the beads to exit from the second size 11° added in Step 1.

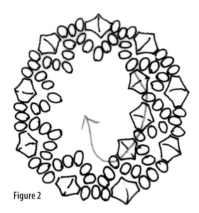

Figure 2

4 Repeat Step 2.

5 Repeat Step 3. Pull everything tight and tie an overhand knot between beads. String 1 size 11°, the 4mm round, 1 rondelle, one 6mm or 8mm round, 1 rondelle, the drop, and 3 size 11°s. Skip the last size 11°s and pass back through all but the first size 11° just strung. String 1 size 11° and pass through the closest size 11° on the wheel. Weave through all the beads to reinforce. Secure the thread and trim. Set the bead-work aside.

6 Use 20" (50 cm) of doubled, waxed thread to string a tension bead. Use size 11°s to work a square of peyote stitch 8 beads wide and 8 beads long. Fold the square so the first and last rows meet and zip the edges. Weave through all the beads to reinforce. Secure the thread and trim. Set aside. Repeat to make fourteen tubes in all.

7 Use beading wire or Power Pro to string 1 crimp tube and half of the clasp. Pass back through the tube, snug the beads, and crimp.

8 String one 6mm or 8mm round, 1 rondelle, 1 peyote-stitched tube, and 1 rondelle seven times. String one 6mm or 8mm round and 1 rondelle. String the Sparkly Wheel by passing the wire through the 3-bead set (1 size 11°, 1 bicone, 1 size 11°) on the outside of the wheel, just opposite the drop. Continue the stringing sequence in reverse to finish the other half of the necklace. String 1 crimp tube, pass through the other half of the clasp and back through the crimp tube. Snug the beads and crimp.

Crochet Braid

Doris Coghill

You don't need to know how to crochet to make this light and fanciful piece.

Materials

Pearls, stone chips, drops or other accent beads

40–60 yd (36–54 m) of 28-gauge wire

2 cones or barrel caps

Two 6mm split rings

Clasp

6" (15 cm) of 20-gauge wire

Tools

Size G or larger crochet hook

Round-nose pliers

Needle-nose pliers

Wire cutters

Techniques

Slipknot, bead crochet, wirework

See pages 119–125 for how-tos

1 Without cutting the wire from the spool, string the beads on the wire. Your bead quantity will depend on how thick you want the finished piece to be.

2 Form a slipknot with the wire. Insert the crochet hook through the loop, leaving a loop of about ½" (1.3 cm). Catch the wire with the crochet hook and pull it back through the loop. The hook should be under the wire. Turn the tip of the hook to the left, catching the wire. Continue turning the hook down and toward you, pulling it back through the loop (Figure 1). This is called a chain stitch.

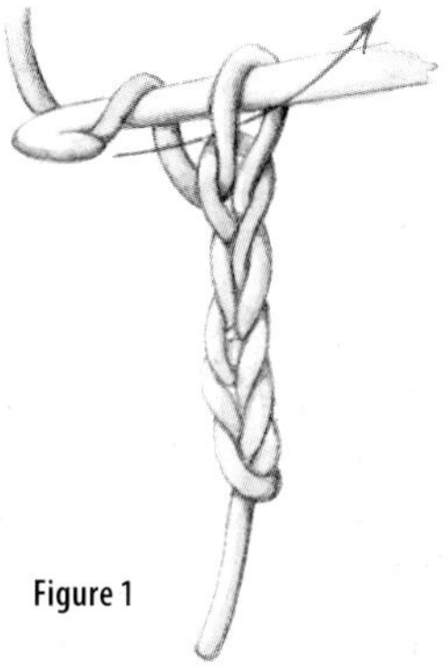

3 Push a bead up so it touches the completed loop and make another chain stitch. Continue alternating plain chain stitches and pushing up beads until the strand is the desired length minus the length of the clasp. Finish the strand with a chain stitch. Remove the hook, leaving the loop, and cut the wire about 5" (12.5 cm) from the stitches. Gently stretch the strand. Repeat to make nine strands in all, each of the same length.

Figure 1

4 Choose one of the following methods to gather the strands together.

Three-braid Method: Gather three of the strands at the end where you started to crochet and lightly twist them together directly above the first chain stitch. Braid the strands together. If the rows strands aren't the same length, adjust by adding or removing stitches and/or beads before you finish the braiding. Repeat twice more, ending up with three braided pieces of the same length. Lightly twist these three pieces together directly above the first stitch and braid the three braids together. Don't twist the braids together so densely that they won't fit into your cone ends.

Single-braid Method: Align all nine strands at the end where you started to crochet and lightly twist them together directly above the first chain stitch. Separate the strands into three groups and braid these groups. If the strands aren't the same length, adjust by adding or removing stitches and/or beads before you finish the braiding.

5 Cut a 3" (7.5 cm) piece of the 20-gauge wire and bend it into a hook shape about ½" (1.3 cm) from the end. Insert the hook into the place you twisted the strands together. Wrap the twisted wire ends of the crocheted strands around the hook several times to secure. Squeeze the hook to secure the twisted ends further, and make a wrapped loop (Figure 2). Continue wrapping the remaining strand ends around the wrapped loop, but test to be sure it will still fit inside the cone pieces you are planning to finish the end with. Trim any excess wire from the twisted strands.

Figure 2

6 String the cone onto the wrapped loop, sliding it down as far as possible so all the strand ends are hidden inside. Make a wrapped loop to secure the cone and strands. Trim any excess wire.

7 Use a split ring to attach one half of the clasp to the wrapped loop just made.

8 Repeat Steps 4–7 to complete the other side of the necklace.

Spiral Sync

Dustin Wedekind

This spiral variation is worked on a prestrung necklace. By using beading wire, you can string larger, heavier beads with small holes without the fear of breaking the thread.

Materials

Size 15° seed beads (A)

Size 11° seed beads (B)

Size 8° seed beads

3mm pearls, stones, or crystals (C)

Large accent beads

Focal bead*

2 crimp tubes

Clasp

Soft Flex .019 beading wire

Beading thread

Tools

Size 12 beading or sharp needle

Crimping pliers

Scissors

Needle-nose pliers

Safety glasses

Techniques

Stringing, modified spiral cord

See pages 119–125 for how-tos

*Shown here: Furnaceworked bead by Connie Haute.

1 Use a crimp tube to attach the beading wire to one half of the clasp.

2 String about 2" (5 cm) of size 8°s and 1 accent bead. Repeat until you reach half of the desired length. You may vary the number of seed beads in each section to make a longer or shorter necklace. String the focal bead. Repeat the size 8° and accent bead stringing sequence to mirror the first side. String 1 crimp tube, pass through the other half of the clasp, pass back through the crimp tube, and crimp.

3 Use 3' (90 cm) of thread to work a spiral cord up the base strand of size 8°s strung in the previous step. Pass through the last size 8° strung on the first half of the necklace, exiting up the strand. String 4A,

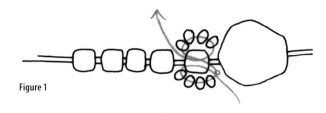

Figure 1

slide the beads down to the necklace, and tie a square knot, leaving a 3" (7.5 cm) tail. Pass through the size 8° again and string 4A. Pass through the same size 8° and the next one down the base strand (Figure 1). Push the loops to the left (you will do this at the end of each step).

4 String 2A, 2B, and 2A and pass through the 2 base beads again. Repeat, passing through the 2 base beads plus 1 more.

5 String 2A, 4B, and 2A and pass through 3 base beads. Repeat, passing through 3 base beads plus 1 more.

6 String 2A, 2B, 1C, 2B, and 2A and pass through 4 base beads. Repeat, stringing 1 size 8° in place of the C and passing through 4 base beads plus 1 more.

7 Repeat Step 5, working two loops over 4 base beads and then shifting up 1 bead to work another two loops over 4 base beads (Figure 2).

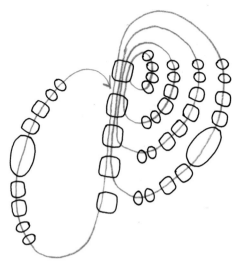

Figure 2

8 When you reach the last 4 base beads before the accent bead, work Steps 2–4 in reverse. After the last A beads are stitched, pass the thread through one of the longer loops exiting the last bead, secure the working and tail threads, and trim.

9 Repeat Steps 2–7 for each section between accent beads. Don't cheat by passing through an accent bead to start the next section—the friction of the heavy bead rubbing against the wire will break the thread. At the end sections near the clasp, pass a loop of seed beads through the clasp to camouflage the crimp and wire. *Note:* If your base beads become too crowded, you can use needle-nose pliers to carefully break one or two of them off the wire. Be sure to wear safety glasses.

Trinket Chain

Jean Campbell

Collect special beads, charms, and lockets to create this special necklace that shows off your wares. It will bring compliments wherever you go.

Materials
Assorted beads and charms
Sterling silver head pins
Sterling silver jump or split rings
26" (65 cm) of heavy sterling silver chain
4" (10 cm) of 20-gauge sterling silver wire

Tools
Wire cutter
Round-nose pliers

Techniques
Stringing, wirework
See pages 119–125 for how-tos

1 Use the silver wire to make a wrapped loop that attaches to the last link of the silver chain. String a bead. Make a wrapped loop that attaches to the other end of the silver chain (Figure 1).

2 String beads on 1 head pin. Make a wrapped loop to secure the beads.

3 Use a jump ring to attach the dangle to one of the chain's links.

4 Repeat Steps 2 and 3 to fill the chain with dangles.

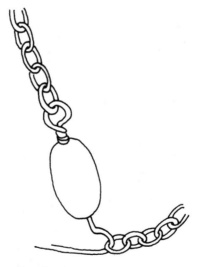

Figure 1

Green Temple

Judi Mullins

This twisting, curving, snakelike necklace is certain to snag attention.

Materials

Size 15°, 11°, 8°, and 6° seed beads
Assortment of 4–8mm pressed-glass, crystal, metal, and semiprecious beads
Focal bead
4 crimp tubes
Clasp
Size D Nymo or Silamide beading thread
20-gauge wire
12" (30 cm) of ¼–⅜" (.6–.9 cm) chain
Soft Flex .019 beading wire
Glue

Tools

Wire cutters
Size 12 beading needle
Scissors
Round-nose pliers
Needle-nose pliers
Measuring tape
Crimping pliers

Techniques

Stringing, wirework, fringe
See pages 119–125 for how-tos

1 Tie a 3' (90 cm) length of thread to the chain, three links in from one end. Glue the knot for extra strength. String 1 size 6° or size 8° and weave through the next link (Figure 1). Repeat down the chain until you reach three links from the other end. Tie a knot to secure the thread. This is the beginning of your base row of beads.

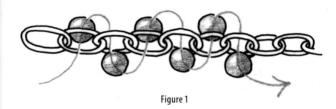

Figure 1

2 Work back toward the beginning of the chain, again adding beads in each link. Don't add the beads in exactly the same place as the first row. Pass back and forth along the chain, adding more beads until you have a full base row to work from.

3 Start a new thread at one end of the base row. Add larger beads by passing through a base-row bead, stringing a large bead, and passing through the next base-row bead. Work down the base row, spacing the large beads down the necklace, and adding smaller beads between the larger ones. Work in three dimensions to keep the diameter of the rope the same all along its width.

4 Continue adding beads along the base row, now using other beads for your anchors rather than always using the base-row beads. Look for spaces where the chain is exposed and cover them with beads. Use smaller and smaller size beads as you create more layers. Work until you have a lush rope with no open holes or gaps. Set the rope aside.

5 Use the 20-gauge wire to string the focal bead and any other beads you might like to add to the center dangle. Cut the wire so it's 2" (5 cm) longer than the length of the beads just strung. Make a wrapped loop at each end of the wire to secure the beads.

6 Use seed beads to make a full tassel of fringe off the loop at the bottom of the center dangle.

7 Attach a piece of thread to the center of the beaded rope where you want your center dangle to hang. Pass the thread through the wrapped loop at the top of the center dangle and attach it securely to the necklace by sewing into the rope and through the wrapped loop several times.

8 Cut the chain so you have only a single link protruding from the bead rope on each end. Use a crimp tube to attach an 8" (25 cm) length of beading wire to the last link on one end of the rope. String a bead with a large enough hole to fit over the crimp tube and snug it against the end of the beaded rope. String an assortment of beads for 4–6" (10–15 cm), depending on how long you want your necklace to be. (These added beads will make up half the length needed to reach your final desired length.) String 1 crimp tube and one half of the clasp. Pass back through the crimp tube, pull the beads snug, and crimp.

9 Repeat Step 8 to finish the other side of necklace.

One-To-Many-Strand Necklace

Diane Fitzgerald

Use a favorite piece of multicolored clothing or a colorful picture as a guide in choosing the bead colors for this lush necklace. Color mixing with seed beads, a process similar to mixing paint, is an important part of the process.

1 Use the piece of clothing or the picture's colors to guide you in assembling small quantities of seed beads in related colors. Mix ¼ to ½ cup (.06 to .12 l) of these beads together in a small dish by adding about a half-teaspoon (2.5 ml) at a time and watching how the color mixture shifts. Next, assemble about 200 small beads, stone chips, rondelles, or size 6° or 8° seed beads in related colors in a separate dish.

2 Cut two 24" (60 cm) pieces of bead cord and fold each of them in half. Place them on a table so the folded ends are 13½" (33.8 cm) apart. Tape the folded ends securely to the table. Point the loops toward each other.

Materials

3 oz size 9° to 11° seed beads in many colors

200–300 small beads, stone chips, rondelles, or size 6° or 8° seed beads

Large, bold, solid-color beads in assorted sizes for necklace strap

2 clamshell bead tips

Clasp

Size D Nymo beading thread

4½' (135 cm) of size F or FF bead cord

Clear nail polish

Fresh beeswax or microcrystalline wax

Tools

Piece of multicolored clothing or a colorful picture

Tape

2 size 12 beading needles

Small sharp scissors

Lighter or thread burner

Pencil

Paper

4" × 4" × 1" (10 cm × 10 cm × 2.4 cm) deep box

12" × 18" (30 cm × 45 cm) piece of cardboard

Techniques

Knotting, stringing

See pages 119–125 for how-tos

3 Cut 9' (27 m) of thread, pass it through a needle, bring the ends together, and make a double overhand knot at the end. Clip the tails close to the knot and melt the knot slightly with a lighter or thread burner. Wax the thread so that the two strands stick together.

4 Use a lark head's knot to attach the thread to one of the cord loops.

5 Randomly string seed beads. After each needle is full, or about 1¼" (3.1 cm) of beads, add a small bead or stone chip. When the length of the strand is exactly long enough to reach the other loop, pass the needle through the loop and back through the last 2–3 beads just strung going in

the opposite direction (Figure 1). Avoid adding a small bead near the bead cord loops because it will interfere with the way the strands hang.

6 Repeat Steps 3–5 until you have the desired number of strands for your necklace, usually twelve to twenty-four strands. Begin new threads as necessary.

7 Remove the tape from one of the bead cords and string 6½" (16.3 cm) of the large beads (both strands go through the large beads). Bring the two ends of the bead cord through a bead tip, tie a square knot, and apply nail polish to the knot. Clip the excess cord and close the bead tip over the knot.

8 Repeat Step 7 for the other cord loop to create the other side of the necklace.

9 Attach one half of the clasp to each bead tip.

Figure 1

Crystal Extravaganza

Melody MacDuffee

The designer, a former tomboy, says she hasn't always been at ease with froufrou styles in her clothing and jewelry. But these earrings gave her the freedom to be as outrageous, glitzy, and uninhibited as she dared to be.

Materials

2 g size 11° gold silver-lined Japanese seed beads

14 light green 3mm Swarovski crystal bicones

42 pink AB 4mm Swarovski crystal bicones

12 light green AB 4mm Swarovski crystal bicones

10 dark green AB 4mm Swarovski crystal bicones

10 dark green AB 6mm Swarovski crystal bicones

6 pale gold AB 6mm Swarovski crystal coins

8 pink AB 6mm Swarovski crystal rounds

8 pink AB 6×10mm AB Swarovski crystal vertically drilled drops

16 gold-filled head pins

2 gold-filled 4mm soldered jump rings

2 gold-filled earring wires

7½' (225 cm) of 24-gauge gold-filled wire

1' (30 cm) of 22-gauge gold-filled wire

2' (60 cm) of fine gauge gold-filled chain

Tools

Chain-nose pliers

Round-nose pliers

Wire cutters

Techniques

Wirework, stringing

See pages 119–125 for how-tos

1. Use the 24-gauge wire to make 1-bead links (a wrapped loop on each side of the bead) for each of the following beads: 4 light green 4mm bicones, 4 dark green 4mm bicones, 8 pink 4mm bicones, 8 pink 6mm rounds, 6 pale gold 6mm coins, and 4 dark green 6mm bicones. Set the thirty-four links aside.

2. Use head pins to make 1-bead dangles (a wrapped loop on one end) for each of the following beads: 4 light green 4mm bicones, 4 dark green 6mm bicones, and 4 pink teardrops. Set the twelve short dangles aside.

3. Use 1 head pin to string 1 pink teardrop, 1 size 11°, and 1 dark green 4mm bicone. Make a wrapped loop to secure. Repeat to make a second long dangle and set both aside.

4. Cut four ⅝" (1.5 cm) lengths of chain and four 2⅜" (6.6 cm) lengths. Set the eight pieces of chain aside.

5. Cut two 1½" (3.8 cm) lengths of 22-gauge wire, two 2½" (6.3 cm) lengths, and two 3½" (8.8 cm) lengths. Use the round-nose pliers to make a simple loop on one end of each wire.

6. Use one of the 1½" (3.8 cm) lengths of wire to string the following links with 1 light green 3mm bicone between each: 1 light green 4mm bicone, 1 dark green 4mm bicone, 4 pink 4mm bicones, 1 dark green 4mm bicone, and 1 light green 4mm bicone. Make a simple loop at the end of the wire to secure the links and beads. If the beads don't fit snugly on

the wire, uncurl the loop, cut off the excess wire, and make another loop.

7 Use one of the 2½" (6.3 cm) lengths of 22-gauge wire to string 1 pink 6mm round. *String 1 size 11°, 1 single link of chain, the bottom loop of the first (next) 4mm bicone from Step 5, 1 single link of chain, 1 size 11°, 1 single link of chain, and 1 coin. Repeat from *, substituting the following links (in order) for the coin: 1 dark green 6mm bicone; 1 pink 6mm round; 1 coin; 1 pink 6mm round; 1 dark green 6mm bicone; 1 coin; 1 pink 6mm round. Make a simple loop at the end of the wire to secure the beads.

8 Use one of the 3½" (8.8 cm) lengths of 22-gauge wire to string the bottom loop of the first link from Step 7, 1 pink 4mm bicone, 1 light green 4mm bicone link, 1 pink 4mm bicone, the bottom loop of the next link from Step 7, 1 pink 4mm bicone, and 1 light green 6mm bicone link. String 1 pink 4mm bicone, the bottom loop of the next link from Step 7, 1 pink 4mm bicone, 1 short teardrop dangle, 1 pink 4mm bicone, the bottom loop of the next link from Step 7, 1 pink 4mm bicone, the long teardrop dangle, and the next link from Step 7. Repeat the stringing sequence for this step in reverse, omitting the long teardrop dangle. Make a simple loop at the end of the wire to secure the beads.

9 Use 2" (5 cm) of 24-gauge wire to form a wrapped loop that attaches to 1 jump ring. String 1 light green 4mm bicone, 1 size 11°, 1 pink 4mm bicone, 1 size 11°, and 1 dark green 4mm bicone. Make a wrapped loop at the other end of the wire that attaches to the end of a ⅝" (1.5 cm) length of chain in the loop. Repeat, using the same jump ring.

10 Open one side loop on the top crossbar of the earring and attach the end link of the chain added in Step 9. Repeat for the second chain. Close the loop securely.

11 Attach one end of a 2¼" (5.6 cm) length of chain to each side loop on the second crossbar of the earring. Close the loops securely.

12 Make sure that the jump rings are at the front of the earring. Attach the earring wire to the jump ring, hooking the top link of the long chains into the earring wire loop as well. You may have to adjust the length of the chains so that the earring hangs at the length desired. If you hook the right-hand chain in first and the left-hand one second for the first earring, do the opposite for the second earring, so that their natural swing is in opposite directions and allows them to lie nicely alongside the face.

13 Use a head pin to string 1 pink teardrop, 1 size 11°, 1 dark green 6mm bicone, 1 size 11°, 1 pink 4mm bicone, and 1 size 11°. Make a wrapped loop that captures the jump ring between the two short chains, leaving about ½" (1.3 cm) of wire exposed at the top.

14 Repeat Steps 6–13 to make the second earring.

Beaded Bead Stiletto

Melody MacDuffee

Suggesting a highly refined look, these stilettos nevertheless pack a wallop as they draw the eye from the ear down to the main event—a beaded bead as dazzling and colorful as you want it to be.

Materials

16 silver-lined size 11° Japanese seed beads

2 clear 12mm glass rounds

92 smoky green AB 3mm fire-polished rounds

52 clear silver-lined 3mm fire-polished rounds

Two 3–4" (7.5–10 cm) lengths of 2mm rounded sterling silver chain

2 sterling silver head pins

2 sterling silver earring posts

Size B white Nymo beading thread

Tools

Size 12 beading needle

Round-nose pliers

Wire cutters

Flat-nose pliers (optional)

Technique

Wirework

See pages 119–125 for how-to

1 Use 3' (90 cm) of thread to string 1 size 11°, 1 green 3mm, 1 silver-lined 3mm, 2 green 3mms, 1 silver-lined 3mm, 1 green 3mm, and 1 size 11°, leaving a 6" (15 cm) tail. This makes up the first strand of the first section.

2 Pass down through the 12mm and through the rest of the beads just strung to attach the strand to the 12mm.

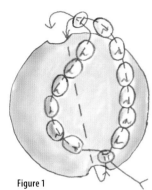

Figure 1

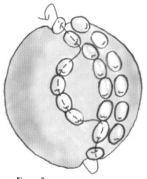

Figure 2

3 Pass down through the 12mm and the first size 11° strung in Step 1. String 1 green 3mm, 1 silver-lined 3mm, 2 green 3mms, 1 silver-lined 3mm, and 1 green 3mm. This makes up the second strand of the first section. Pass through the last size 11° strung in Step 1 (Figure 1).

4 Pass down through the 12mm and the first size 11° of the first strand. Pass through the first green 3mm of the second strand. String 1 silver-lined 3mm, 2 green 3mm, and 1 silver-lined 3mm. Pass through the last green 3mm on the second strand and the last size 11° on the first strand (Figure 2). This makes up the third strand of the

first section. Pass through the last size 11° strung in Step 1 (Figure 2).

5 Using the same working thread, repeat Steps 1–4 three times to make a total of four sections around the 12mm. If the beads don't completely cover the base bead, add another one or two strands like the third strand to fill the gap.

6 Use 1 head pin to string 1 green 3mm and the beaded bead. Make a wrapped loop that attaches to the bottom link of one length of chain. Connect the ear post to the other end of the chain.

7 Repeat Steps 1–6 to make the second earring.

Chained Reflection

Joanie Jenniges

These earrings are simple, chic, and fun, and they take advantage of the earring nut—a jewelry finding that's often ignored. Try the suggested earrings here or experiment with your own color combinations and a variety of crystal shapes and sizes.

Materials

4 tanzanite 4mm Swarovski crystal cubes
4 tanzanite 6mm Swarovski crystal cubes
8 black diamond 2× AB 4mm Swarovski crystal bicones
4 sterling silver 1" (2.5 cm) head pins (.25–.28 thick)
12 sterling silver 1" (2.5 cm) eye pins (.25–.28 thick)
2 sterling silver 5.5mm jump rings
2 sterling silver 4mm earring ball posts with loops and winged ear nut backings
33-link length of sterling silver 2.2 mm flat cable chain

Tools

Chain-nose pliers
Round-nose pliers
Flush cutters

Techniques

Stringing, wirework
See pages 119–125 for how-tos

1 Cut the chain into six pieces with two links each and eight pieces with one link each. Set aside.

2 String one 6mm cube on a head pin and make a simple loop close to the cube. Repeat with the three remaining 6mm cubes to make four dangles in all. Set aside.

3 String one 4mm cube on an eye pin and make a simple loop close to the cube. Repeat with the three remaining 4mm cubes to make four links in all. Set aside.

4 String 1 bicone on an eye pin and make a simple loop close to the cube. Repeat with the seven remaining bicones to make eight links in all. Set aside.

5 Open the loop on the ball post, attach a two-link piece of chain, and close the loop. Attach a bicone link to the end of the chain. Attach a two-link chain piece to the end of the bicone link. Attach a bicone link to the end of the chain. Attach a one-link chain piece to the end of the bicone link. Attach a 4mm cube link to the end of the chain. Attach a two-link chain piece to the end of the cube link. Attach the 6mm cube dangle to the end of the chain.

6 Open a jump ring and attach it to one of the loops of the earring nut; close the jump ring. Attach a bicone link to the jump ring. Attach a one-link chain piece to the end of the bicone link. Attach a cube link to the end of the chain. Attach a one-link chain piece to the end of the cube link. Attach a bicone link to the end of the chain. Attach a one-link chain piece to the end of the bicone link. Attach a cube dangle to the end of the chain.

7 Repeat Steps 5 and 6 to make the second earring.

Crystal Elegance

Joanie Jenniges

Experimenting with moss stitch produced this pretty double-sided, three-dimensional design that employs Swarovski crystals. With or without the drops, they work up quickly.

Materials

Size 11° Japanese seed beads

Size 14° Japanese seed beads

8 semiprecious stone 3×5mm tubes

16–21 Swarovski crystal 4mm bicones

2 Swarovski crystal 6mm bicones

2 sterling silver or gold-filled earring wires

2 sterling silver or gold-filled 1½" (3.8 cm) head pins (.25–.28 thick)

5' (150 cm) 4 lb extra-fine Fireline or size B Nymo beading thread

Beeswax or synthetic beeswax

Tools

Size 12 beading needle

Scissors

Round-nose pliers

Chain-nose pliers

Wire cutters

1 Use 2½' (75 cm) of thread to string 4 tubes (beads 1–4), leaving a 12" (30 cm) tail. Tie a knot to form a diamond shape. Pass through all the tubes again, exiting from bead 4 so that the working thread, tail thread, and knot are all between the first and fourth tubes. Consider the corners of the diamond as a compass, with a North, South, East, and West.

2 String 1 size 11° and pass through bead 1. String 1 size 11° and pass through bead 2. String 1 size 11° and pass through bead 3. String 1 size 11° and pass through bead 4. Exit from the first bead added in this step (Figure 1).

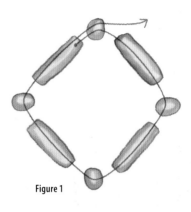

Figure 1

3 String one 4mm, 1 size 11°, and one 4mm. Pass through the West size 11°. Pass back through the last 4mm, size 11°, and 4mm just strung. Pass through the North size 11°, bead 1, and the East size 11°.

4 String one 4mm. Pass through the size 11° strung in Step 3 (doing so will seat the size 11° at the center of the diamond). String one 4mm. Pass through the South size 11°. Pass back through the last 4mm, the size 11° at the center of the diamond, and the first 4mm just strung. Pass through the East size 11°, bead 2, and the South size 11° (Figure 2).

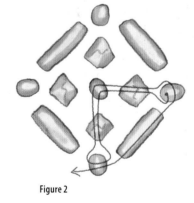

Figure 2

5 Work the back of the earring. Repeat Steps 3 and 4, keeping in mind that the East and West size 11°s, beads 1 and 4, and beads 2 and 3 are now in reversed positions. Turn the work over to the front.

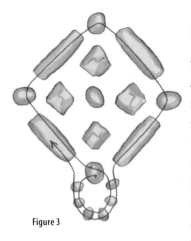

Figure 3

6 If you wish to add drops, string 6 size 14°s. Pass through the South size 11° and all the beads strung in this step. Pass through the South size 11°, bead 3, the West size 11°, bead 4, the North size 11°, bead 1, the East size 11°, and bead 2. Pass back through the beads added in this step (in a clockwise direction). Pass through bead 3 (Figure 3).

7 Weave the working thread through the beadwork to reinforce. Secure the thread and trim.

8 Use the tail thread to pass through the North size 11°. String 3 size 14°s, one ear wire, and 3 size 14°s. Pass through the North size 11° and the beads and ear wire added in this step. Pass through the North size 11° and bead 1. Weave the tail thread through the beadwork. Secure the thread and trim.

9 If you've set up your beadwork for a drop (Step 6), string 1 size 11°, one 6mm, and 1 size 11° on a head pin. Make a simple loop on the head pin so it is immediately above the size 11°. *Note:* The loop must be large enough to fit around the size 14°s added in Step 6. Suspend the dangle from the size 14° loop at the bottom of the earring.

Variation

For the 3-drop earring shown, make 3 crystal dangles. For one of the dangles place the loop ⅜" (1.1 cm) from the top of the crystal. Suspend the dangles from the size 14° loop at the bottom of the earring with the longer dangle placed between the shorter ones.

10 Repeat Steps 1–9 to make the second earring.

Watermelon Balls

Anna Karena

Watermelon tourmaline is a beautiful semiprecious stone that has a range of green, white, and red shades. Instead of actual tourmaline, however, this clever design features bicone crystals in an array of those same shades. The crystals successfully mimic the stone, and they're much easier to find.

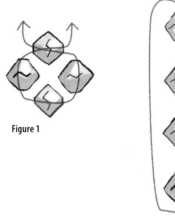

Figure 1

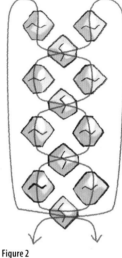

Figure 2

Materials

8 satin jonquil 4mm Swarovski bicones
8 satin light rose 4mm Swarovski bicones
8 satin peridot 4mm Swarovski bicones
2 clear fuchsia 4mm Swarovski bicones
2 green tourmaline 4mm Swarovski bicones
2 sterling silver 2" head pins
2 sterling silver earring wires
24" (61 cm) of Illusion cord

Tools

Scissors
Round-nose pliers
Chain-nose pliers
Side cutters

Techniques

Right-angle weave, stringing, wirework
See pages 119–125 for how-tos

1 Cut 12" (30.5 cm) of cord and hold both ends, one in each hand. String 1 jonquil bicone and slide it to the middle of the cord.

2 Use the left cord end to string 1 light rose bicone and 1 jonquil bicone. Use the right cord to string 1 peridot bicone and pass back through (cross through) the jonquil bicone last strung so the cord crosses within that bead (Figure 1). Doing so will create a diamond shape with the beads.

3 Repeat Step 2 until you've woven 12 bicones in all. End by crossing through the first jonquil bicone strung in Step 1 to create a circle of beads.

4 Tie a half hitch knot between beads and pass through another to hide the knot. Make three more knots with each cord end to secure the beads. Trim the cord close to the work. Set aside.

5 Use 1 head pin to string 1 fuchsia bicone, the beadwork completed in Step 3, and 1 green tourmaline crystal. Make a wrapped loop to secure the beads. Attach the dangle to an earring wire.

6 Repeat Steps 1–5 to make the second earring.

Stardust Earrings

Linda Richmond

Create these dazzling earrings using ladder and herringbone stitch in the round. They're fun to make—and even more fun to wear on a starry evening.

Materials

Size 11° seed beads in two colors (A and B)

32 fire-polished 3mm rounds (C)

32 fire-polished 3mm rounds (D)

Size B beading thread in color to match beads

2 earring wires

Beeswax or synthetic beeswax

Tools

Size 12 beading needle

Chain-nose pliers

Techniques

Ladder stitch, herringbone stitch

See pages 119–125 for how-tos

1 Use 3' (90 cm) of doubled, waxed thread to make a strip of ladder stitch 16A long, leaving a 6" (15 cm) tail. Stitch the first and last beads together to form a foundation circle.

2 Use A to work a round of herringbone stitch off the foundation circle. As you work, hold the beadwork flat (Figure 1). The foundation circle will eventually flatten out completely. Exit up through the first bead added in this round.

3 String 1C, 1B, and 1C. Pass down through the next bead stitched in Step 2, as you would for herringbone stitch. String 1B and pass up through the

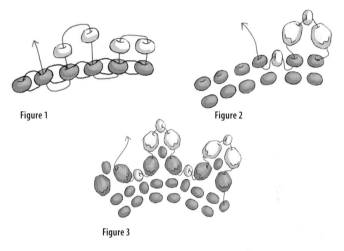

Figure 1

Figure 2

Figure 3

next bead stitched in Step 2 (Figure 2). Repeat around the circle. Exit up through the first 3mm added in this round.

4 String 1D, 1B, and 1D. Pass down through the next 3mm stitched in Step 3. String 1B and pass up through the next 3mm stitched in Step 3 (Figure 3). Repeat around the circle. Exit up through the first 3mm and size 11° added in this round.

5 String 4B. Pass through the last size 11° added in Step 4 again to make a loop. Weave through these 5 beads again to reinforce. Secure the thread and trim. Attach the earring wire to the loop just made.

6 Repeat Steps 1–5 to make the second earring.

Sheer Dangles

Heidi Presteen

Wondering what to do with leftover beads? These earrings will inspire mixes and matches that make an enchanting pair of drop earrings.

Materials

16 semiprecious stone chip beads
34 small accent beads
16 thin sterling silver eye pins
34 thin sterling silver head pins
2 sterling silver earring wires

Tools

Round-nose pliers
Chain-nose pliers
Flush cutter

Techniques

Stringing, wirework
See pages 119–125 for how-tos

1 Use an eye pin to string 1 chip. Make a simple loop to secure the chip. Repeat seven times to make eight links in all.

2 Open one of the loops on a link made in Step 1. Attach it to an earring wire and close the loop. Open a loop on a second link and attach it to the bottom of the link just added. Close the loop. Continue adding links until you have a chain of eight. Set aside.

3 Use 1 head pin to string 1 accent bead. Make a simple loop to secure the bead. Repeat sixteen times to make seventeen dangles in all.

4 Use a chain-nose pliers to open the loop on one of the dangles. Attach the three dangles to the bottom loop on the chain made in Step 2. Continue to add the dangles to the connector chain, adding one dangle to each loop on the chain.

5 Repeat Steps 1–5 to make the second earring.

Sparkly Studs

Jean Campbell

If you like to wear your earrings close to the lobe, try this design. They are quick to make, and it's fun to experiment with different bead colors.

Materials

Size 11° seed beads

12 size 8° triangle beads

Two 8mm earring posts with flat faces for gluing

Size B Nymo beading thread in color to match beads

E-6000 adhesive

Tools

Size 12 beading or sharp needle

Scissors

Toothpick

Technique

Peyote stitch

See pages 119–125 for how-to

1 Create a beaded dome with circular peyote stitch.

Round 1: Use 2' (60 cm) of thread to string 3 size 11°s, leaving a 4" (10 cm) tail. Tie a knot to form a circle. Exit through the first bead strung.

Round 2: String 1 size 11° and pass through the second size 11° added in Step 1. String 1 size 11° and pass through the third size 11° added in Step 1. String 1 size 11° and pass through the first size 11° added in Step 1 and the first size 11° added in this round.

Round 3: String 1 triangle and pass through the next size 11° added in the previous round. Repeat around to add three triangles in all (Figure 1). Exit from the first triangle added in this round.

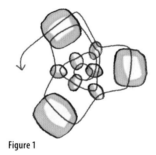

Figure 1

Round 4: String 2 size 11°s and pass through the next triangle added in the previous round. Repeat around to add 6 size 11°s in all (Figure 2). Exit from the next triangle added in the previous round.

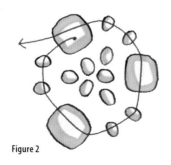

Figure 2

Round 5: String one triangle and pass through the next triangle from Round 3. Repeat around to add three triangles in all. Exit from the first triangle added in this round.

Round 6: String 3 size 11's and pass through the next triangle added in the previous round. Repeat around to add 9 seed beads in all (Figure 3). The beadwork should begin to cup into a dome. Weave through all the beads in the piece again to tighten and reinforce. Pass through the first 3 size 11's strung in this round and the next triangle.

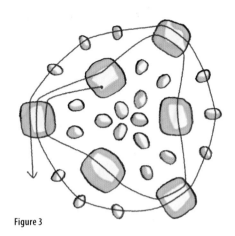

Figure 3

Round 7: String 5 size 11's and pass through the next triangle added in Round 5. Repeat around to add 15 seed beads in all (Figure 4). The beads added in this round will frame the beads added in Round 6. Weave through all the beads added in this round again. Secure the thread and trim.

2 Use a toothpick to apply glue to the inside/back of the beadworked dome, taking care not to let the glue ooze out to Round 7. Apply the beadwork to the face of the earring finding.

3 Repeat Steps 1 and 2 to make the second earring.

Figure 4

Briolette Earring Jackets

Christine Prussing

Here's a way to use beads to perk up a pair of gemstone or pearl stud earrings. Just add the "jacket" to the stud before you put them on. The mesmerizing way that crystals emerge from a rocky matrix was the inspiration for this pair of line earrings.

Materials

Size 11° crystal/black-striped Czech seed beads
Size 12° gold-lustered hex-cut Japanese seed beads
Size 15° gold-lustered Japanese seed beads
2 cut lead crystal 10×7mm briolettes
12' (3.6m) of 8 lb moss green PowerPro beading thread
2 gold-filled or 14K soldered 4.5mm round jump rings
Masking tape

Tools

2 size 12 beading needles
Sharp scissors
Thread burner
Optivisor or other type of magnifier (optional)

Techniques

Lark's head knot, right-angle weave
See pages 119–125 for how-tos

1 Fold 6' (18m) of thread in half. Pass the fold through the middle of a jump ring, and back over the jump ring. Pull the pair of tails to tighten the fold to make a lark's head knot around the jump ring (Figure 1).

Figure 1

2 Attach a needle to each end of the thread, leaving 8" (20 cm) tails on each end.

3 Work a vertical row of thirteen units of two-needle right-angle weave, following the pattern of alternating diagonal stripes of the size 11° and larger cut beads (Figure 2). Tack the jump-ringed end down with a bit of masking tape to hold the row in place as you work.

4 Make the last unit of the row by stringing 1 size 11° and 4 size 15°s on the left needle. Pass through the first size 15° just strung again and string a cut bead. Use the right needle to cross back through the cut bead last strung. This step creates a picot of size 15°s at the end of the row.

Figure 2

5 On the left needle, string 1 briolette and 2 size 11°s. Cross the right thread back through the last bead strung.

6 Rotate the beadwork to match Figure 3. Pass the right thread back through the adjacent cut bead from Step 4. String 4 size 15°s. Pass through the last size 15° strung again. Pass through the 2 size 11°s from Step 5 again.

Figure 3

85

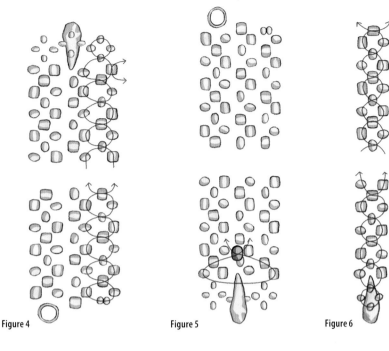

Figure 4

Figure 5

Figure 6

er thread through the briolette, up through the size 11° bead on the opposite side (Row 1), and string a size 11° bead. Cross the other thread through the last bead strung. Tighten carefully to curl the edges of the work upward.

Create the final 4-bead picot by passing one thread back through the seed beads of the previous unit as in Step 6.

7 Work the row upward, making alternating diagonal stripes. For the final unit, pass through the adjacent size 11° of Row 1, string 2 cut beads, and cross the other thread through the last cut bead.

8 Rotate the beadwork to match Figure 4. This row will be the front of the earring jacket. Because gemstone studs often flare outward from front to back, this row starts with 2 size 15° beads in order to make the jacket front short enough to fit against the stud. String 2 size 15°s beads, 1 size 11°, and 1 cut bead. Cross the other thread through the cut bead.

9 Work the row upward, making alternating diagonal stripes. Create the 4-bead picot at the end by passing through the adjacent size 11° on Row 2. String 4 size 15°s and pass through the first size 15° just strung again. String 1 cut bead and cross the other thread through the cut bead just strung.

10 Rotate the beadwork and flip it over to match Figure 5; the threads should emerge from the cut bead on the lower right side. This row zips together the edges of Rows 1 and 3. Pass the low-

11 Continue to zip up the jacket by following Figure 6. After the final unit, pass one thread through the beads at the top of the jacket, through the jump ring, and down through the bead on the corner of the back side. Pass the other thread through the jump ring, down through the bead on the near corner of the back side, and through the top middle bead of the back side. Tie a square knot and pass one end back through the middle bead to hide the knot. Weave through the beads downward and tie knots inside the middle beads of the next two units. Use the thread burner to invisibly trim the ends.

12 Repeat all steps to make the second earring jacket. *Note:* To create a reverse spiral in the second jacket, follow the pattern for the first jacket, only flip the work over before you create the picot at the base of Row 2. Then flip the work back again to match the diagram and continue as for the first jacket. The briolette will appear to rest atop the picot at the base of Row 2. Do not flip the work over at the start of Row 4. The threads will emerge from the cut bead at the lower left of the work. Proceed as in Step 10, but pass the lower thread through the briolette from left to right instead.

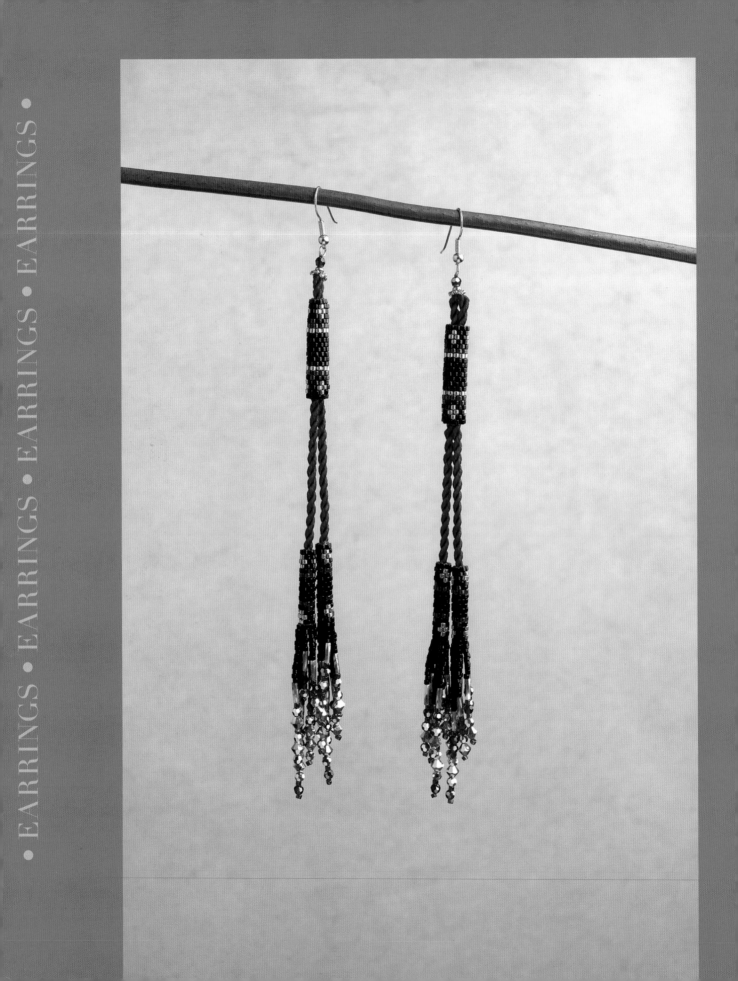

Shooting Stars

Betcey Ventrella

If you know how to work flat peyote stitch, you'll be able to make these unique earrings. Put them on and let the celestial show begin!

Materials

5 g opaque black Delica beads (DB-010)

2 g 24K bright gold Delica beads (DB-031)

2 g garnet gold-luster Delica beads (DB-105)

24 size 2 bright gold bugle beads

24 aurum gold 2×4mm Swarovski bicones

24–30 aurum gold 2×3mm Swarovski rounds

24–30 Siam satin 3mm Swarovski rounds

2 gold-filled ear wires

2 gold-filled bead caps

Two 1' (30 cm) pieces of 2mm twisted cotton burgundy cord

Size B burgundy Nymo beading thread

Fray Check

Hypo Cement

Masking or clear tape

Tools

Size 12 beading needle

Scissors

Techniques

Peyote stitch, fringe

See pages 119–125 for how-tos

Figure 1

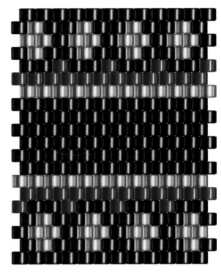

Figure 2

1 Fold one of the cord pieces in half. Tape the cord together near the fold (Figure 1). Add Fray Check to the cord ends and let dry. Set aside.

2 Following the chart (Figure 2), work peyote stitch to make a rectangle 20 beads wide by 12 beads long.

3 Fold the beadwork made in Step 2 over the taped area on the cording. Bring the first and last rows of the beadwork together and zip the edges. Carefully insert the glue applicator between the cord and the beadwork. Apply enough glue to attach the beadwork firmly to the cord. Let dry.

4 Following the chart (Figure 2), work peyote stitch to make two rectangles 15 beads wide by 6 beads long.

5 Fold one of the pieces of beadwork made in Step 4 over one end of the cording. Bring the first and last rows of the beadwork together and zip the edges. Glue the beadwork to the cord as before. Let dry. Repeat this step for the remaining cord end.

6 Weave to the bottom of one beaded tube (the edge farthest away from the cord fold). String 5 black Delicas, 1 garnet Delica, 1 bugle, 1 garnet Delica, 1 Siam round, 1 garnet Delica, 1 gold round, and 1 garnet Delica. Skipping the last bead strung, pass back through all the beads and up through the last bead exited on the tube. Pass down through an adjacent bead at the end of the tube. Continue around to make a fringe leg for each bead at the bottom of the tube. Follow Figure 3 to make the pattern seen here or create a design of your own.

7 Repeat Step 6 for the other cord end.

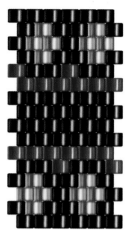

Figure 2

8 Secure a knotted thread to the top of the folded cord. String 1 bead cap, 1 Siam round and the loop of an ear wire. Pass through all several times again to reinforce. Secure the thread and trim.

9 Repeat all the steps to make the second earring.

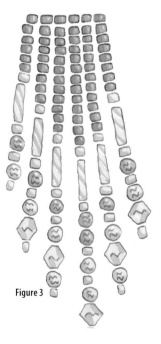

Figure 3

Czech Cab Earrings

Doris Coghill

Tiny cabochons are the perfect centerpieces for these embroidered earrings. When the designer found the vintage cabs during a trip to the Czech Republic, she knew they were destined for her ears.

Materials

2 g size 15° seed beads (A)

1 g size 15° seed beads (B)

1 g size 15° seed beads (C)

Two 5×8mm cabochons

2 pieces of 1½"×1½" felt

2 pieces of 1"×1" Ultrasuede

2 earring wires

Size D Nymo thread in color to match beads

Silicone-based glue

Tools

Size 12 beading or sharp needles

Scissors

Techniques

Bead embroidery, edging

See pages 119–125 for how-tos

1 Use glue to attach one cabochon to the middle of a piece of felt. Don't let the glue leak past the edges of the cabochon or your needle will not be able to pierce the felt where there is dry glue.

2 Tie a knot at the end of 3' (90 cm) of thread. Take a small stitch under the cabochon on the back side of the felt. Bring the thread up through the felt as close to the edge of the cabochon as possible.

3 Work backstitch embroidery around the cabochon.

Round 1: String 3A. Push the beads down the thread so they are touching the felt and lying along the edge of the cab. Pass down through the felt at the end of the third bead.

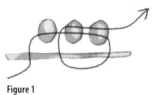

Figure 1

Pass back up through the felt between the first and second bead and through the second and third bead (Figure 1). Repeat around the cab. For the last stitch, string as many beads as needed to fit in the space to complete the round. Pass back through all beads in the round to make them line up neatly. Pass down through the felt and back up next to the completed round of beads in order to start the next round.

Round 2: Work backstitch using B.

Round 3: Work backstitch using C. When the round is completed, pass through the felt. Take a small stitch on the back to anchor the thread. Tie an overhand knot but don't cut the thread.

4 Trim the felt even with the edge of the last row of beads, being careful not to cut your working thread or the threads on the back of the felt.

5 Use glue to attach the trimmed piece to a piece of suede. Exit the working thread from between the two layers. Allow the glue to set for about 30 minutes and then trim the piece of suede the same size as the felt.

6 Take a small stitch through the suede and the felt very close to the edge, moving from back to front. Before pulling the loop of thread tight, pass the needle through the loop to form an overhand knot.

7 String 3A. Working from back to front, pass the needle through both layers about one bead's width from the knot. Pass up through the last bead strung (Figure 2). String 2A. Working from back to front, pass the needle through both layers about one bead's width from the last bead anchored. Pass back up through the last bead strung. The beads touching the fabric should be sitting side by side with their edges touching. Repeat around the perimeter of the earring. Finish the round of edging by stringing 1A and passing down through the first bead strung in this step. Take another small stitch to anchor the edging and tie an overhand knot.

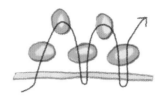

Figure 2

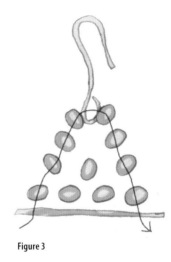

Figure 3

8 Find the three edging beads located at the center top of the earring. Weave through the beads and exit from either the left or right bead of the edging stitch. String 2A, the ear wire, and 2A. Skipping the center edging bead, go through the next one (Figure 3). Pass the needle through the two layers of fabric at the edge of the earring and back up into the beads just added. Repeat at least twice more to reinforce the loop.

9 Pass between the layers of fabric and exit between any two rounds of bead embroidery. Secure the thread and trim.

10 Repeat Steps 1–9 to make the second earring.

Retro Wraps

Jennifer Sevlie Diederich

This spirited look from the 1960s and 1970s is made new again with up-to-date color choices. By wrapping the large drop with an assortment of beads on wire you'll make your own statement.

Materials

Size 6°, 8°, and 11° seed beads in color to match the top-drilled beads
4mm Swarovski crystal bicones or triangle beads
2 top-drilled 15×40mm elongated drop beads
2 earring wires
24" (61 cm) of 26-gauge wire

Tools

Round-nose pliers
Side cutters

Techniques

Stringing, wirework
See pages 119–125 for how-tos

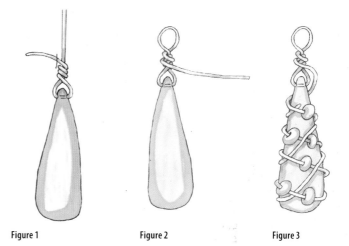

Figure 1   Figure 2   Figure 3

1 Cut a 12" (30.5 cm) piece of wire and insert it through a top-drilled bead from left to right, leaving about 3" (7.5 cm) on the right side.

2 Bend the right-side wire up and around the top of the bead. Bend the left-side wire up and around the top of the bead and straight up to form a spine for a wire bail. Wrap the right-side wire around the spine three times. Trim with the side cutters (Figure 1).

3 Use a round-nose pliers to make a loop with the spine wire. Wrap this wire down the spine to meet the existing wire wrap (Figure 2).

4 String an assortment of beads on the remaining wire. Move a few beads toward the large bead and wrap the wire around it. Continue moving a few beads toward the large bead and wrapping the wire randomly around it until you have 3" (7.5 cm) of wire left. Weave the remaining wire back up through the beads to hold them in place and hide the wire end. Trim the wire when you reach the top of the large bead (Figure 3).

5 Attach the dangle to an earring wire.

6 Repeat Steps 1–5 to make the second earring.

Inner Light Ring

Jeannette Cook

Inspired by those wonderful Miyuki color-lined teardrop beads, this gorgeous ring is designed to wow your admirers. Show off your inner power with pride!

Materials

Orange color-lined Miyuki drops

Olive Delica beads

Red Delica beads

½ of a cotton ball

1"×1" (2.5×2.5 cm) piece of white grosgrain ribbon

Orange size B Nymo or Silamide beading thread

Beeswax or Thread Heaven

Tools

Size 12 beading needle

Scissors

Pen

Lighter or thread burner

Technique

Peyote stitch

See pages 119–125 for how-to

1 Draw a circle about the size of a quarter on the ribbon. Use 3' (90 cm) of doubled and conditioned thread to sew a running stitch on the line you just made on the ribbon. Cut around the circle about ⅛" (.3 cm) from the stitching. Use the lighter or thread burner to carefully singe the frayed edges.

2 Pull the ends of the thread to slightly draw in the sides of the circle, making the ribbon cup. Roll the cotton ball in your fingers to tighten it and stuff it into the cup. Continue pulling the thread to tighten it around the cotton ball. Use the scissors end to tuck any loose cotton back into the ribbon as you tighten it. Gather the seam outside the stitching and tack it down neatly. Rub this end on a flat surface to make it as flat as possible.

3 Pass the needle up through the top center of the ribbon. String 1 drop and pass back down through the ribbon, close to where you last exited. Pull tight to seat the drop close to the ribbon. Continue stitching drops in concentric circles as tightly together as possible until you have covered all but the flattened end of the ribbon ball. Set aside.

4 Use 3' (90 cm) of single conditioned thread and olive Delicas to work a piece of peyote stitch 14 beads wide and 8 beads long. Work 4 more rows, decreasing on each side of the beadwork until you're left with 6 beads across. Weave through the beads to the first row created in this step and make identical decreases. This piece will be the platform for the ring top.

5 Use red Delicas to work a 6-bead-wide band of peyote stitch off the platform created in Step 4. Work until the beadwork fits comfortably around your finger.

6 Zip the end of the band to the other side of the platform. Weave through all the beads on the band to reinforce, finishing near the center of the platform.

7 Center the beaded ribbon ball on the platform and securely stitch it into place. Secure the thread and trim.

Crystal Visions Ring Band

Susan J. Manchester

This sparkly crystal band is a great off-loom project for first-timers. Put it on and no one will know how easy it was to make!

Materials

12 Swarovski crystal 4mm bicones
Metallic-finish size 11° seed beads
4 lb monofilament fishing line

Tools

Size 10 beading needle
Scissors

Techniques

Netting and peyote stitch variations
See pages 119–125 for how-tos

1. Use 3' (90 cm) of line to string 5 size 11°s. String 1 bicone and 1 size 11° five times. String 1 bicone.

2. String enough size 11°s so that all of the strung beads fit comfortably around your finger. (For ring sizes 5–6, string 20 size 11°s to complete the band; for sizes 7–8, 23 size 11°s; for sizes 9–10, 26 size 11°s.) Tie the beads to form a circle, leaving a 6" tail.

Note: It's important to keep the tension tight as the beads are worked into the ring band. When working the band in Row 2, keep working on the same side of Row 1. Don't flip the work. Refer to Figure 1 for the stringing path.

3. Pass back through the first 2 beads strung in Step 1.

4. String 3 size 11°s and 1 bicone. Pass through bead 6 (marked on Figure 1).

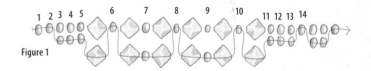

Figure 1

5. String 1 bicone, 1 size 11°, and 1 bicone. Pass through bead 8. String 1 bicone, 1 size 11°, and 1 bicone. Pass through bead 10.

6. String 1 bicone and 3 size 11°s. Pass through bead 14.

7. String 2 size 11°s. Skip the next 2 size 11°s in the band and pass through the next size 11°. Continue stringing 2 size 11°s, skipping 2, and passing through the next one in the circle until the band is completed.

8. Weave through all of the beads to reinforce. Secure the thread and trim.

Beaded Cluster Ring

Lisa Gettings

Here's a cocktail ring for the twenty-first century! Large and funky, it's perfect to make on a Saturday afternoon just before heading out to dance the night away.

Materials

16–20 fire-polished or Swarovski crystal 4mm rounds

1' (30 cm) of sterling silver 14-gauge wire or purchased ring band

1 spool of nontarnish silver 24-gauge Artistic Wire

G-S Hypo Cement

Tools

Flush cutters

Chain-nose pliers

Ring mandrel

Technique

Wirework

See pages 119–125 for how-to

1 Wrap the 14-gauge sterling silver wire around the ring mandrel at a half size larger than your ring size. Overlap the wire where it overlaps by about one-third of the circumference of the ring and cut (Figure 1).

2 Use 3' (90 cm) of 24-gauge wire to secure the overlapped section by leaving one end of the wire several inches longer than the other and wrapping it tightly around the overlap (Figure 2). The longer length of wire will be used to make the ring top. Place a few drops of glue on the wrapped section and let dry.

If you use a purchased ring band, cut 3' (90 cm) of 24-gauge wire, leaving one end of the wire several inches longer than the other, and wrap tightly around the "top" of the ring band.

3 String 1 bead on the long piece of wire. Anchor it about ¼" (.6 cm) above the wrapped base by bending the wire down on each side of the bead. Twist the bead and wire two to three times while holding down the long length of wire in place. This will firmly anchor the bead on top of the base (Figure 3).

Figure 1   **Figure 2**

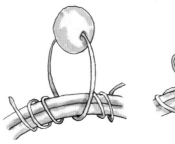

Figure 3

4 Wrap the wire one time around the base to further secure the bead and string another bead. Repeat the twist-and-wrap process across the entire wrapped base, making sure to place the beads in a clustered pattern.

5 When you are pleased with the shape and beads added to the base, anchor the ends of the remaining wire between the beads. Find a tight spot and weave the wire carefully around several beads. Trim the wire close to the ring, making the ends as inconspicuous as possible.

6 Cut 2' (60 cm) of 24-gauge wire. Anchor one end of the wire at one end of the beaded cluster. Wrap the wire tightly and uniformly along the rest of the bare base to the other side of the beaded cluster. Neatly anchor the wire and trim.

Stone, Set, Match

Anna Karena

Who says you can't set stones amidst beadwork? This design marries the more traditional look of set stones and free-form beadwork. The result? A whimsical ring with the touch of opulence.

Materials

Delica beads

Assorted accent beads (seed beads, bugle beads, 4mm fire-polished beads and crystals, small pearls, stones, and sterling silver pieces)

Faceted flat-backed gemstone

Prong setting

Size B Nymo or Silamide beading thread in color to match the Delicas

Tools

Size 12 beading needles

Scissors

Chain-nose pliers

Techniques

Peyote stitch, brick stitch, bead embroidery, fringe

See pages 119–125 for how-tos

1 Set the faceted stone by placing it into the prong setting and squeezing the prongs with the pliers.

2 Use 3' (90 cm) of thread and Delicas to work a strip of flat peyote stitch 14 beads wide and 7 beads long. This will be the platform for the ring's top. Weave through the beads to exit from the fifth bead (make sure it's a bead that sticks "up") along the last row you stitched so your needle passes toward the center of the beadwork.

3 Continue working peyote stitch off the beadwork you created in Step 2, but this time work only 6 beads wide and long enough so that all of the beadwork wraps comfortably around your finger. Match the beadwork to the middle of the opposite side of the piece created in Step 2 and zip the edges to complete the band.

4 Exit from the place on the platform that you'd like to set your stone. Place your setting on the bead-work and pass through a prong. Pass down through a bead underneath the prong and weave through to the bead underneath the next prong. Continue around the setting to tack it down, always hiding your thread within the beads on the platform. Exit from a bead next to the setting.

5 String 1 Delica, lay it flat on the platform, and pass through the beads that make up the platform, exiting from a bead near to where you entered. Repeat around the setting to make a tight bezel. To further secure the setting, pass through the prongs as you go.

6 Work a round of peyote stitch off the beads you added in Step 5. If needed to reach the top of your setting, work more rounds of peyote stitch. When you are even with the top of the setting, work one more round of peyote stitch, this time making two or three decreases. Pull the thread tight so the beadwork further secures the setting. Weave through the beads to the platform.

7 Work the rest of the ring top in a free-form fash-ion. Be creative as you add larger beads or dif-ferent shapes to the platform using peyote or brick stitch, fringe, or other embroidery stitches. Because the platform is so small, it's good to keep in mind that every bead is important. Small accents of color go a long way in your total design. Size 15° beads are especially useful to tuck away in small corners or add a punch of color. When finished embellishing, secure your thread and trim.

Buttercup

Betcey Ventrella

This lovely flower ring seems a little tricky to make at first, but once you've got the hang of it you can easily make one for each finger.

Materials

Size 11° seed beads in color to match crystals
5 Swarovski crystal 4mm rounds
5 Swarovski crystal 4mm bicones
5 Swarovski crystal 6mm lentils
2 crimp tubes
Fireline
4" (10 cm) of .05mm Stretch Magic jewelry elastic

Tools

Size 12 beading needle
Scissors
Crimping pliers
Beading tweezers

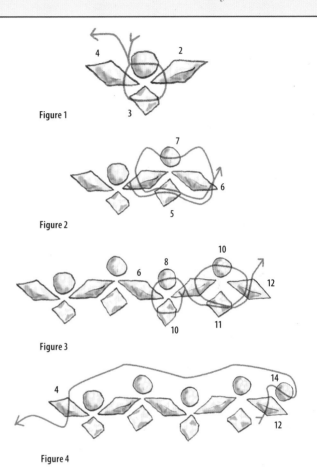

Figure 1

Figure 2

Figure 3

Figure 4

1 Use 4' (120 cm) of thread to string 1 round, 1 lentil, 1 bicone, and 1 lentil. These are beads 1–4 on Figure 1. Pass through all again, exiting from bead 4. Tie a knot and trim the tail end close to the work. Pass through beads 1 and 2 again to clear the knot.

2 String 1 bicone (bead 5), 1 lentil (bead 6), and 1 round (bead 7). Pass through beads 2, 5, and 6 (Figure 2).

3 String 1 round (bead 8), 1 lentil (bead 9), and 1 bicone (bead 10). Pass through beads 6, 8, and 9 (Figure 3). String 1 bicone (bead 11), 1 lentil (bead 12), and 1 round (bead 13). Pass through beads 9, 11, and 12 (Figure 3).

4 String 1 round (bead 14) and pass through bead 4 to form a circle (Figure 4).

5 String 1 bicone (bead 15) and pass through beads 12 and the last bicone (Figure 5). Reinforce and tighten the circle by passing through the all the bicone crystals once. Pass through one of the lentils, and reinforce and tighten the round crystals by passing through all of them once.

6 String 5 seed beads, skip the next round crystal, and pass through the next one. Continue around the circle, making "petals" (Figure 6). Once you've added seed beads around all 5 crystals, reinforce by passing through all again. Exit from the second seed bead added in this step.

7 String 3 seed beads and pass through the fourth seed bead added in Step 6. Pass through the next 3 seed beads so you exit from the second seed bead of the next petal (Figure 7). Repeat around to add 5 picots in all. Reinforce by passing through all the seed beads.

8 If your flower is still floppy at this point, reinforce by passing up through one of the lentils, through the adjacent bicone, and back down through the next lentil. Pass through the round crystal, back up the next lentil, through the adjacent bicone, and so on. Weave to the seed bead petals and to the second bead added in Step 6.

9 String 6 seed beads and pass through bead 4 (see Figure 7). Reinforce by passing through all just strung. Weave to the opposite side of the flower. Because this is a five-petal flower, there isn't an exact opposite, so you'll have to improvise a bit in deciding which seed beads to exit from. Add 6 seed beads on this side as you did on the other. Weave through a few more beads, secure the thread, and trim.

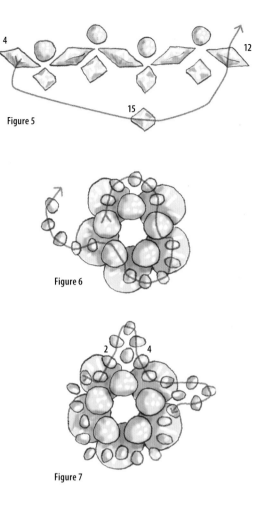

Figure 5

Figure 6

Figure 7

10 Use the elastic to string 1 crimp tube. Pass the end through one of the loops created in Step 9, then back through the crimp tube leaving a ½" (1.3 cm) tail. Squeeze the tube neatly and tightly using crimping pliers and trim the short tail close to the tube.

11 String about 20–30 seed beads onto the elastic. Because it is difficult to string the size 11's on the elastic, use a beading tweezers to pick the seed beads one at a time to place them on the end of the elastic. Test the fit around your finger and adjust accordingly. String 1 crimp tube, pass through the other loop created in Step 9, and back through the crimp tube. Pull all snug, crimp neatly, and trim.

Wonder Dome Ring

Susan J. Manchester

Create this elegant ring using bicone crystals to weave half of a dodecahedron—who thought geometry could be so fun? To make this sparkly math class a little easier, visualize making three interlocking flowers when you work the dome; each flower contains five petals and five seed beads in the center.

Materials
Metallic-finished size 11° seed beads
18 Swarovski crystal 4mm bicones
Spiderline or 4 lb Fireline

Tools
Size 10 beading needle
Scissors

1 Use 6' (180 cm) of line to string 1 crystal and 1 seed bead three times, leaving an 8" (20 cm) tail. Tie a knot to form a circle. Pass through the first 5 beads again, exiting from the third crystal just strung.

2 String 1 seed bead, 1 crystal (marked on Figure 1 as bead 4), 1 seed bead, 1 crystal (bead 5), and 1 seed bead. Pass through bead 3 (Figure 1). *Note:* To reinforce the weave, do another pass through the beads added in this step, bead 3, the next seed bead, and bead 4. Make this second pass when adding new beads in the following steps.

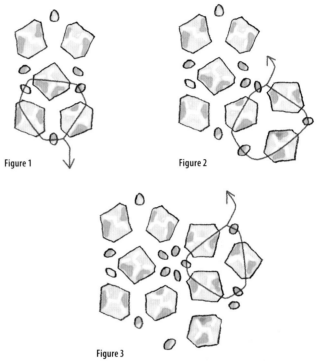

Figure 1

Figure 2

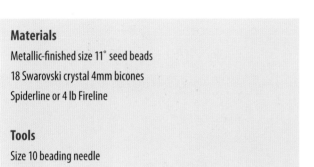

Figure 3

3 String 1 seed bead, 1 crystal (bead 6), 1 seed bead, 1 crystal (bead 7), and 1 seed bead. Pass through bead 4, the next seed bead, bead 6, the next seed bead, and bead 7 (Figure 2).

4 String 1 seed bead, 1 crystal (bead 8), 1 seed bead, 1 crystal (bead 9), and 1 seed bead. Pass through bead 7, the next seed bead, and bead 8. You now have five petals of your first flower.

5 String 1 seed bead, 1 crystal (bead 10), and 1 seed bead. Pass back through bead 1. String 1 seed bead and pass through bead 8, the next seed bead, and bead 10 (Figure 3). This step gives you the fifth "seed" in the center of your five-petal flower.

6 String 1 seed bead, 1 crystal (bead 11), 1 seed bead, 1 crystal (bead 12), and 1 seed bead. Pass through bead 10 (Figure 4). Weave through the beads to exit at bead 12.

7 String 1 seed bead, 1 crystal (bead 13), 1 seed bead, 1 crystal (bead 14), and 1 seed bead. Pass through bead 12, the next seed bead, and bead 13 (Figure 4).

8 String 1 seed bead, 1 crystal (bead 15), and 1 seed bead. Pass through bead 9. String 1 seed bead and pass through bead 13 (Figure 4). Pass through the first seed bead added in this step and bead 15 to create the fourth petal of the last flower.

9 String 1 seed bead, 1 crystal (bead 16), 1 seed bead, 1 crystal (bead 17), and 1 seed bead. Pass through bead 15, the next seed bead, and bead 16 (Figure 4).

10 String 1 seed bead, 1 crystal (bead 18), and 1 seed bead. Pass through bead 6. String 1 seed bead and pass through bead 16 (Figure 4). Pass through the first seed bead added in this step and bead 18.

11 Exiting from bead 18, string 3 seed beads. Pass through the next crystal and adjacent seed bead on the perimeter of the dome. String 1 seed bead and pass through the next seed bead and crystal on the perimeter of the dome. Repeat this step twice around the dome (Figure 4). Weave through all the beads again to reinforce. Pass through a set of three seed beads on the perimeter.

12 Create a band by stringing the number of seed beads required to fit your finger. The number of beads should be a multiple of 3, plus 1 (e.g., 31, 34, 37, etc.).

13 Pass through the 3 matching seed beads on the opposite side of the dome. String 3 seed beads and pass through the fourth-to-last bead strung in Step 12. String 2 seed beads, skip 2 beads on the band, and pass through the next. Continue stringing 2 beads and skipping 2 beads until there are 3 beads left on the band. String 3 seed beads and pass through the set of 3 seed beads you last passed through in Step 11. Weave through all the beads on the band twice more to reinforce. Secure your thread and trim.

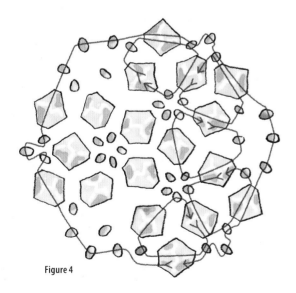

Figure 4

Lucky Scrunchie Ring

Jamie Hogsett

This ten-minute project will get you hooked on making rings! It is flashy and stylish, but also easily glides over any finger, making it very comfortable.

Materials

44 sterling silver 4mm heishi spacers
2 sterling silver 6mm Swarovski crystal rondelles
1 Swarovski crystal 8mm round
1 sterling silver 1mm crimp tube
6" (15 cm) of clear .05mm stretch elastic

Tools

Chain-nose pliers or crimping pliers

Technique

Stringing
See pages 119–125 for how-to

1 Use the elastic to string 22 spacers, 1 rondelle, 1 round, 1 rondelle, and the remaining spacers.

2 String the crimp tube and pass through the first several spacers you strung in Step 1. Gently pull both ends of the elastic to snug all the beads. Crimp the tube using the chain-nose or crimping pliers. Trim both ends close to the crimp tube.

Simplicity Ring

Sandy Amazeen

If you have swollen knuckles and have sworn off ring-wearing, this knitted ring made with stretch cord is the answer to your prayers! And making one just might inspire you to use up that bead soup piling up on a corner of your beading table.

Materials
A bead mixture that includes size 6° and 8° seed beads, 4mm accent beads, minidrops, and minidaggers
16 matching small accent beads
1 spool of 0.5mm clear stretch cord
Silamide thread to match the beads

Tools
4" (10 cm) size 0 double-pointed knitting needles
Zap-A-Gap or other quick-drying super glue
Big Eye needle
Beading needle

Technique
Bead knitting
See pages 119–125 for how-to

Note: These instructions assume a basic knowledge of bead knitting.

1 String 20" (50 cm) of assorted beads from the bead mixture onto the cord. Tie an overhand knot and fit it snugly onto one of the knitting needles. Add a drop of glue to the knot and allow it to dry. Cast on three stitches, sliding 3 beads between each stitch.

2 Knit a row, sliding 3 beads down to the working needle with each stitch. Some of the beads may slide out of place, but these won't show in the finished ring.

Continue to knit row by row until the piece fits comfortably around your finger. Cast off the three stitches and weave the ends of the ring together using a Big Eye needle and the cord. Draw these stitches together so that the ring narrows a bit at the join. This slightly narrower section will create a comfortable fit at the underside of the finger. Add a drop of glue to the knot. Using the Big Eye needle, weave the tails and trim the ends.

3 Thread 24" (60 cm) of double-stranded Silamide onto the beading needle. Find the top center of the ring. Count two raised rows from the center and secure the thread.

4 Pass through a seed bead, string 1 accent bead and 1 seed bead. Pass back through the accent bead. Pass through two adjacent beads on the base of the ring. Repeat until you have embellished the ring with 3 beads per row for 5 rows. Secure the thread and trim.

Sister Lucien

Betcey Ventrella

When you wear this ornate ring you'll receive more compliments than you'll know what to do with! But it's not just pretty, it's smartly constructed. The top is made with thread that just won't break, and the elastic cord band makes it very comfortable.

Materials

2 g of size 15° seed beads

20 size 11° seed beads to match ring top

1 Swarovski crystal 9×6mm oval

12 Swarovski crystal 3mm rounds

2 crimp tubes

Fireline

4" of .05mm Stretch Magic jewelry elastic

Tools

Crimping pliers

Size 12 sharps or beading needles

Beading tweezers

Scissors

Techniques

Tension bead, picots

See pages 119–125 for how-tos

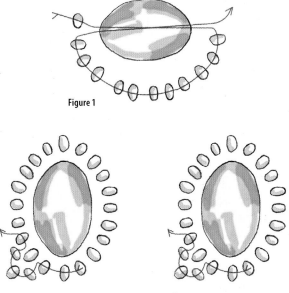

Figure 1

Figure 2   Figure 3

1 Use 4' (120 cm) of thread to string a tension bead, leaving a 4" (10 cm) tail. String 1 size 15°, the oval crystal, and 11 size 15°s.

2 Skip the first size 15° and pass through the crystal (Figure 1). String 11 size 15°s and pass through the first seed bead strung in Step 1 to form a ring of seed beads around the crystal.

3 Reinforce the entire circle of seed beads by passing through each size 15° twice. Trim the tail and tension bead.

4 Pass through one of the seed beads, string 3 size 15°s, skip 1 seed bead on the base round, and pass through the next seed bead (Figure 2). Repeat around the circle to make 12 picots (Figure 3). Exit from the second bead of one of the picots.

5 String 1 round crystal and pass through the next picot tip. Continue around to add 12 crystals in all.

6 String 1 size 15° and pass through the next round crystal. Repeat around the circle (Figure 4). Exit from one of the size 15°s added in this step.

7 String 4 size 15°s and pass through the next size 15° added in Step 6. Repeat around the circle (Figure 5). Reinforce by passing through all the size 15°s in this outer round. Exit from the second size 15° in a set added in this round that's found at the side of the crystal oval. It's here you'll begin the ring band.

8 String 6 size 15°s and pass through the second size 15° added in the next set. Reinforce the loop and secure the thread. Weave through the beads to the other side of the ring top and repeat this step. Trim the thread.

9 Cut a 4" (10 cm) piece of elastic and string 1 crimp tube. Pass the elastic through the middle of one of the seed bead loops created in Step 8 and pass back through the tube. Gently crimp the tube and trim the tail close to the tube.

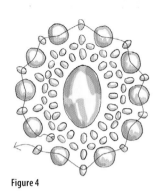

Figure 4

Figure 5

10 String enough size 11°s so the ring top and band fit comfortably around your finger. Because it's difficult to string the size 11°s on the elastic, use a beading tweezers to pick the seed beads one at a time to place them on the end of the elastic. String 1 crimp tube, pass through the other loop created in Step 8, and back through the tube. Pull all snug, crimp neatly, and trim.

{Techniques}

General How-Tos

Finishing and Starting New Threads

Tie off your old thread when it's about 4" long by making a simple knot between beads. Pass through a few beads and pull tight to hide the knot. Weave through a few more beads and trim the thread close to the work. Start the new thread by tying a knot between beads and weaving through a few beads. Pull tight to hide the knot. Weave through several beads until you reach the place to resume beading.

Gluing

Place a sparing amount of glue on knots to secure them (G-S Hypo Cement or clear nail polish works well) or use enough glue to completely secure beads to a surface (E6000, Terrifically Tacky Tape). Allow any glue to dry thoroughly before continuing. Seal large glue-beaded surfaces with Mod Podge.

Pass Through vs Pass Back Through

Pass through means to move your needle in the same direction that the beads have been strung. Pass back through means to move your needle in the opposite direction.

Tension Bead

String a bead larger than those you are working with, then pass through the bead one or more times, making sure not to split your thread. The bead will be able to slide along but will still provide tension to work against when you're beading the first two rows.

Bead Crochet

Insert the hook into the back of the stitch, put the yarn over the hook, and draw a loop through—you now have two loops on the hook. Slide a bead up to the loops, wrap yarn over the hook, and draw the yarn through the loops. The bead will be fixed to the back side of the work.

Bead Knitting

Insert the needle into the stitch to be knitted as with regular knitting. Slide the bead up against the needle, then pull the bead through to the front as you complete the stitch. If you want beads in every row, you will have to work in the round or cut the thread at the end of each row so that you are always working on the same side of the piece.

Edgings

Simple Edging

To begin, secure the thread in the beadwork or fabric. String 3 beads and pass through the beadwork or fabric about 1 bead's width away from where you exited. Pass back through the last bead strung. String 2 beads and pass through the beadwork or fabric about 1 bead's width away from where you last exited. Pass back through the last bead strung. Continue across, adding 2 beads at a time.

Fringes

Simple

String a length of beads plus 1 bead. Skipping the last bead, pass back through all the beads just strung to create a fringe leg. Pass back into the foundation row or fabric.

Leaf

Step 1: String the desired length of vine-colored beads and 6 leaf-colored beads. Pass back through the second-to-last bead strung.

Step 2: String 3 leaf-colored beads. Pass back through the first leaf-colored bead strung in Step 1 and all of the vine-colored beads.

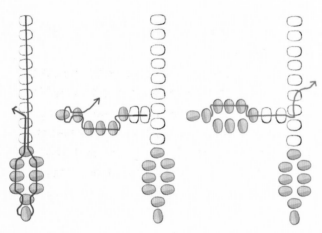

Knots

Lark's Head Knot

Lark's head knots are great for securing stringing material to a cord or bar. Begin by folding the stringing material in half. Bend the fold over the bar (Figure 1). Pull the ends through the loop and tighten (Figure 2).

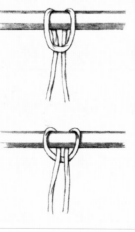

Overhand Knot

Make a loop with the stringing material. Pass the cord that lies behind the loop over the front cord and through the loop. Pull tight.

Square Knot

First make an overhand knot, passing the right end over the left end. Next, make another overhand knot, this time passing the left end over the right end. Pull tight.

Surgeon's Knot

The surgeon's knot is very secure and therefore good for finishing off most stringing materials. Tie an overhand knot, right over left, but instead of one twist over the left cord, make at least two. Tie another overhand knot, left over right, and pull tight.

Off-Loom Stitches

Bead Embroidery (backstitch)

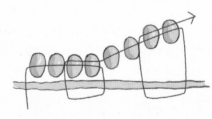

Begin by passing through the fabric, from wrong side to right side. String 4 beads. Lay the beads against the fabric and pass down through it just past the fourth bead. Pass up through the fabric between the second and third beads and pass through the last 2 beads just strung. String 4 beads and repeat.

Brick Stitch

Begin by creating a foundation row in ladder stitch or using a secured thread. String 2 beads and pass under the closest exposed

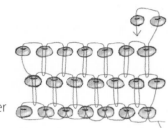

loop of the foundation row and back through the second bead. String 1 bead and pass under the next exposed loop and back through the bead just strung; repeat.

To decrease within a row, string 1 bead and skip a loop of thread on the previous row, passing under the second loop and back through the bead.

To increase within a row, work two stitches in the same loop on the previous row.

Ladder Stitch

Thread a needle on each end of the thread, and pass one needle through 1 or more beads from left to right and pass the other needle through the same beads from right to left. Continue adding beads by crisscrossing both needles through 1 bead at a time. Use this stitch to make strings of beads or as the foundation for brick stitch.

To work a single-needle ladder stitch, string 2 beads and pass through them again. String 1 bead. Pass through the last stitched bead and the one just strung. Repeat, adding 1 bead at a time and working in a figure-eight pattern.

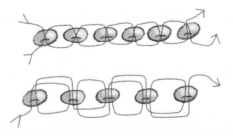

Netting

Begin by stringing a base row of 13 beads. String 5 beads and pass back through the fifth bead from the end of the base row. String another 5 beads, skip 3 beads of the base row, and pass back through the next. Repeat to the end of the row, passing through the fifth, fourth, and third beads of those just strung and exiting from the third. Turn the work over and go back across the same way.

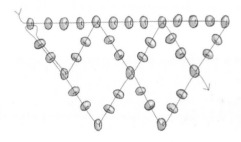

Tubular Netting

String 1A and 1B six times; pass through them again to form a circle for the foundation round. *String 1A, 1B, and 1A; skip 1B and pass through the following 1B in the previous round. Repeat from * twice, then step up for the next round by passing through the first 2 beads of this round. Work each round the same way.

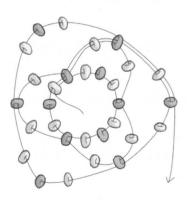

Peyote Stitch

Flat Peyote Stitch

One-drop peyote stitch begins by stringing an even number of beads to create the first two rows. Begin the third row by stringing 1 bead and passing through the second-to-last bead of the previous rows. String another bead and pass through the fourth-to-last bead of the previous rows. Continue adding 1 bead at a time, passing over every other bead of the previous rows.

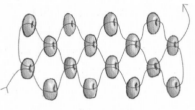

Two-drop peyote stitch is worked the same as above, but with 2 beads at a time instead of 1.

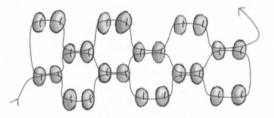

To make a mid-project decrease, simply pass thread through 2 beads without adding a bead in the "gap." In the next row, work a regular one-drop peyote over the decrease. Keep tension taut to avoid holes.

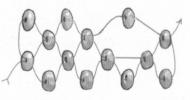

To make a mid-project increase, work a two-drop over a one-drop in one row. In the next row, work a one-drop peyote between the two-drop. For a smooth increase, use very narrow beads for both the two-drop and the one-drop between.

"Zipping" or "zipping up" a piece of flat peyote stitch entails folding the beadwork so the first and last rows match. The beads should interlock like a zipper. (If the beads don't interlock, add or subtract one row from the beadwork.) Pass through 1 bead of the first row and the next bead of the last row, lacing the beads together, to create a seamless tube.

Circular Peyote Stitch

Begin by threading 3 beads and pass back through the first bead to form a circle. For the second round, add 2 beads and pass through the second bead of the first round, add 2 more beads and pass through the third bead of the first round, then add 2 more beads and pass back through the first bead of the first round and the first bead of the second round. For the next round, add 1 bead and pass through the second bead of the second round, add 1 bead and pass through the third bead of the second round, and so on, adding 1 bead between every 2 of the previous round. Continue in this manner, alternating the two rounds.

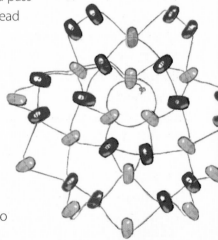

Tubular Peyote Stitch

String an even number of beads and make a foundation circle by passing through them two more times, exiting from the first bead strung. String 1 bead and pass through the third bead of the foundation circle. String 1 bead and pass through the fifth bead of the foundation circle. Continue adding 1 bead at a time, skipping over 1 bead of the first round, until you have added half the number of beads of the first round. Exit from the first bead of the second round.

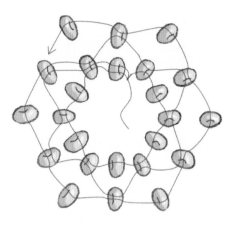

String 1 bead, pass through the second bead added in the second round, and pull thread tight. String 1 bead and pass through the third bead added in the second round. Continue around, filling in the "spaces" 1 bead at a time. Exit from the first bead added in each round.

Right-Angle Weave

Single Needle

String 4 beads and pass through them again to form the first unit. For the rest of the row, string 3 beads, pass through the last bead passed through in the previous unit, and the first two just strung; the thread path will resemble a figure eight, alternating directions with each unit. To begin the next row, pass

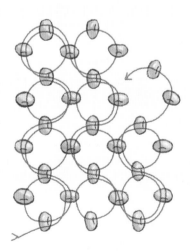

through the last 3 beads strung to exit the side of the last unit. String 3 beads, pass through the last bead passed through, and the first bead just strung. *String 2 beads, pass through the next edge bead of the previous row, the last bead passed through in the previous unit, and the last 2 beads just strung. Pass through the next edge bead of the previous row, string 2 beads, pass through the last bead of the previous unit, the edge bead just passed through, and the first bead just strung. Repeat from * to complete the row, then begin a new row as before.

To make a row-end decrease, weave thread through the second bead added in the second-to-last group from the previous row. Begin the new row by stringing 3 beads. Pass back through the first bead added in the second-to-last group from the previous row. Pass through the beads just added. Continue across the row, adding 2 beads at a time.

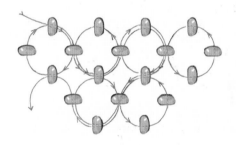

To make a row-end increase, begin a new row as usual, exiting thread from the third bead just added. String 3 beads. Pass back through the third bead added in the last set (making a figure eight). Weave to the first bead added in this set and continue across the row, adding 2 beads at a time.

Double Needle

Using one needle on each end of the thread, string 3 beads to the center of the thread. *Use one needle to string 1 bead, then pass the other needle back through it. String 1 bead on each needle, then repeat from * to form a chain of right-angle units (A).

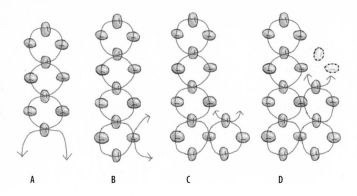

A   B   C   D

To turn at the end of the row, use the left needle to string 3 beads, then cross the right needle back through the last bead strung (B). Use the right needle to string 3 beads, then cross the left needle back through the last bead strung (C). To continue the row, use the right needle to string 2 beads; pass the left needle through the next bead on the previous row and back through the last bead strung (D).

Square Stitch

Begin by stringing a row of beads. For the second row, string 2 beads, pass through the second-to-last bead of the first row, and back through the second bead of those just strung. Continue by stringing 1 bead, passing through the third-to-last bead of the first row, and back through the bead just strung. Repeat this looping technique to the end of the row.

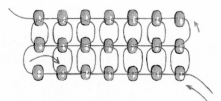

To make a decrease, weave thread through the previous row and exit from the bead adjacent to the place you want to decrease. Continue working in square stitch.

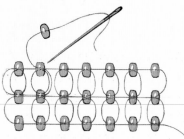

To make an increase, string the number of beads at the end of the row you want to increase. Work the next row the same as the previous row.

Spiral Cord

String 4 size 8° seed beads and 5 size 11° seed beads. Pass through the size 8° beads again. *String 1 size 8° and 5 size 11° beads. Pass through the last 3 size 8°s and the size 8° just strung. Repeat from * until you reach the desired length. *Note:* The beads used for this cord can be varied. Just be sure that the length of the "outer" bead strand is never shorter than the larger "core" bead strand.

Stringing

Stringing is a technique in which you use a beading wire, needle and thread, or other material to gather beads into a strand.

Crimping

Begin the strand of beads with a crimp tube. Pass through the clasp or connector. Pass back through the crimp tube and, if possible, a few beads on the strand. Snug the crimp tube and beads close to the closure. Spread the two wires so they line each side of the tube. Use the first notch on the crimping pliers (round on one jaw, dipped on the other) to squeeze the crimp tube shut, making sure there's one wire on each side of the crimp. Use the second notch on the crimping pliers (rounded on both jaws) to shape the tube into a tight round. Make gentle squeezes around the tube for a perfect cylinder. Trim the tail wire close to the beads.

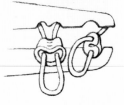

Button-and-Loop Clasp

General instructions are given here to show how to make the clasp, but you may need to modify the number of seed beads to tailor the clasp to your specific button or large bead.

Step 1: Use a shank button to make an anchor for the clasp. To start, measure enough beading wire to complete a one-strand necklace or bracelet. String 1 crimp tube and the button. Pass back through the crimp tube.

You can also use a bead (9mm or larger) to act as the anchor for your clasp. To begin this technique, measure enough beading wire to complete a one-strand necklace or bracelet. String 1 crimp tube, the large bead, and 1–3 seed beads. Pass back through the large bead and the crimp tube and crimp.

Step 2: String enough seed beads so that as you lay the strand across the back of the shank button, the end reaches the edge of the button. If you are using a large bead as the anchor, string 1–5 seed beads.

Step 3: String the beads for the body of the necklace or bracelet.

Step 4: String 3 seed beads and 1 crimp tube. String enough seed beads so that when you pass back through the crimp tube the loop slides snugly over the button or large bead. Remove or add seed beads as necessary, pass back through the crimp tube, snug all the beads, and crimp.

Wireworking

Coil

Use one hand to hold the end of your wire against a mandrel. With the other hand, wrap the wire around the mandrel in tight loops. To remove the coil, slide it off the mandrel and cut. Add vertical loops on either end to use the coil as is, or cut the coil at certain intervals to make jump rings or split rings.

Loops
Simple loop

To form a simple loop, use flat-nose pliers to make a 90-degree bend at least ½" from the end of the wire. Use round-nose pliers to grasp the wire after the bend; roll the pliers toward the bend, but not past it, to preserve the 90-degree bend. Use your thumb to continue the wrap around the nose of the pliers. Trim the wire next to the bend. Open a simple loop by grasping each side of its opening with a pair of pliers. Don't pull apart. Instead, twist in opposite directions so that you can open and close without distorting the shape.

Wrapped Loop

To form a wrapped loop, begin with a 90-degree bend at least 2" from the end of the wire. Use round-nose pliers to form a simple loop with a tail overlapping the bend. Wrap the tail tightly down the neck of the wire to create a couple of coils. Trim the excess wire to finish. Make a thicker, heavier-looking wrapped loop by wrapping the wire back up over the coils, toward the loop, and trimming at the loop.

Opening Jump Rings

Jump rings are most often used to connect wirework to findings. When you open a jump ring, use two pliers and bend the ends laterally, not apart. Add the finding and close the jump ring with the two pliers. Be sure to close the jump ring completely so that your finding doesn't slip out. Do so by closing the ends slightly farther than where the ends match up—the wire will spring back to the right position.

Spiral

To start a spiral, make a small loop at the end of a wire with round-nose pliers. Enlarge the piece by holding on to the spiral with chain-nose pliers and pushing the wire over the previous coil with your thumb.

{Contributors}

Sandy Amazeen is a frustrated painter who taught herself weaving, spinning, knitting, stained glass, and jewelry making while traveling the continent. What refuses to come out of her head to appear on canvas is coaxed to life through a number of other outlets including beadwork, which she has enjoyed for more than thirty years.

Dona Anderson-Swiderek is the author of the self-published books *Beading Heart Designs: Amulet Purses* and *Let's Face It*. Find Dona's teaching schedule on her website, http://members.tripod.com/~beadingheart.

Sharon Bateman lives in North Idaho, and has been beading professionally since the early nineties. She can be reached for questions or comments at www.sharonbateman.com.

Lilli Brennan, a resident of East Strouds-burg, Pennsylvania, has been designing wire and bead jewelry in conjunction with WigJig for the past several years. A passionate jewelry lover all her life and a crafter in many media, she finds the most satisfaction in producing beautiful, delicate pieces.

Jean Campbell is a craft author and editor whose specialty is beading. She is the founding editor of *Beadwork* magazine and has written and edited several books, including *The New Beader's Companion* (with Judith Durant), *Getting Started Stringing Beads,* and *Beaded Weddings* (all Interweave Press). Jean lives in Minneapolis with her family and a whole lot of beads.

Doris Coghill has been a beader for many years and has been involved with some type of craft all her life. She is currently busy with designing and teaching beadwork and working with her business, Dee's Place. She can be reached at www.beadsbydee.com.

Jeannette Cook has been working with beads as a wearable and fine art form for thirty-five years and teaching beading workshops for eighteen years. She is owner of Beady Eyed Women and can be reached at www.beadyeyedwomen.com.

Jennifer Sevlie Diederich has been working and teaching at The Bead Monkey in St. Paul, Minnesota, for the past several years, and she loves being surrounded by so many creative people, ideas, and BEADS.

Margo C. Field "discovered" beads in 1990. After retiring from a career in hospital pharmacy, she opened Poppy Field Bead Company in Albuquerque, New Mexico. She teaches classes at her store and workshops across the United States.

Diane Fitzgerald is a bead artist, writer, and teacher who lives in Minneapolis, Minnesota. She had written several books, including *Beading with Brick Stitch*, *Netted Beadwork*, and *Beaded Garden* (all Interweave Press). Diane can be reached at dmfbeads@bitstream.net.

Lisa Gettings lives in Seattle and credits her mother, Linda, a frequent project contributor to *Beadwork* magazine, for her addiction to beading.

Jeri Herrera has been beading for over a decade and teaches beading in her local community. Jeri can be reached at jeri@dbeadmama.com or www.dbeadmama.com.

Jamie Hogsett is editor of *Stringing* magazine and author of *Stringing Style* (Interweave Press). She works with beads, plays with beads, and lately inhales beads as they are taking over her house.

{Resources}

The beads and supplies used in this book are widely available through local and online bead shops, bead shows, and mail order catalogs.

ArtBeads.com
(866) 715-2323
www.artbeads.com
One reason to shop Artbeads.com is their great selection of all kinds of beading materials, but the free shipping is an added bonus.

Beadalon
(866) 423-2325
www.beadalon.com
(wholesale only)
You can't directly buy spools of Beadalon's beading wire, tools, or findings, but their helpful website can put you in touch with a shop that can.

The Bead Monkey
3717 West 50th Street
Minneapolis, MN 55410
www.thebeadmonkey.com
One of the finest bead shops in the country, you'll find all of your basics at The Bead Monkey.

Beadsmith
37 Hayward Avenue
Carteret, NJ 07008
(732) 969-5300
www.beadsmith.com
Wholesale Only
Beadsmith is a family-run company that carries just about anything you need in the way of beading materials.

Beyond Beadery
PO Box 460-BW
Rollinsville, CO 80474-0460
(800) 840-5548
www.beyondbeadery.com
They are known for their great selection of Swarovski crystals, but another treasure is their myriad of seed beads for sale.

Fire Mountain Gems
(800) 355-2137
One Fire Mountain Way
Grants Pass, OR 97526-2373
www.firemountaingems.com
FMG is usually the first place a new beader goes to shop online. And there's a reason--they have everything!

Joanie Jenniges, with the support of her husband and four children, shares her passion for beadwork through designing and teaching. She lives in Minnesota and can be reached at joaniejenniges@comcast.net or www.beadworkdesigns.com.

Anna Karena lives in Minneapolis, Minnesota, and is the manager of a bead store. Contact her at annakarena@mac.com.

Melody MacDuffee has been making jewelry for many years, at first exclusively with crochet, and then gradually expanding her love of her tiny hooks and beads to a love of equally tiny beading needles and lengths of wire. She is widely published in bead and crochet publications and teaches a variety of techniques in her classes.

Susan J. Manchester is a corporate executive from Mound, Minnesota, who is eagerly awaiting retirement so she can spend more time beading and teaching bead classes.

Pat Mayer has discovered many joys that have come to her through beading, such as the love of the creative process, the beauty of the beads, the fun of the hunt, and the wonderful friendships made with kindred spirits she has met along the beading path.

Judi Mullins has been doing beadwork off and on for most of her adult life. She has been published in several magazines and has taught around the Northwest. You can contact her at bead.garden@verizon.net.

Lisa Norris is a self-taught beadworker with a degree in chemical engineering, which she hasn't used since her kids were born.

Theresa Grout Ostertag has been a jewelry designer since 1992 and a glass beadmaker since 1993. She has had a lifelong passion for seed beads and loves to incorporate them into her jewelry along with her own handmade glass beads. She can be reached through her website www.rebeads.com.

Heidi Presteen's favorite beads are crystals and pearls. She also enjoys hunting for crafty treasures, golfing, and summer weather.

Chris Prussing owns a bead shop in Juneau, Alaska, and is the author of *Beading with Right Angle Weave* (Interweave Press, 2004).

Linda Richmond of Sandpoint, Idaho, has been captivated by beads for most of her life, and she launched a full-time beading career in 1995. She sells her kits, along with beads, tools, books, and supplies, through her website at www.lindarichmond.com.

Ellen Sadler is thrilled to have found the perfect creative outlet sized for New York City apartments. She may be reached at ellensadler@juno.com.

Jane Tyson is a Tasmanian beadwork teacher and bead seller. She can be contacted at jrtyson@netspace.net.au.

Betcey Ventrella is the all-knowing goddess of Beyond Beadery in Rollinsville, Colorado. Contact her at (303) 258-9389; betcey@beyondbeadery.com; www.beyondbeadery.com.

Dustin Wedekind is the senior editor of *Beadwork* magazine where he is also known as "Bead Boy." A seed-beader for over ten years, Dustin finally succumbed to the "fancy beads" only recently.

Lucky Gems
www.lucky-gems.com
Wholesale Only
For the wholesaler, Lucky Gems stocks an incredible selection of unique beads.

Ornamental Resources
Box 3303
Idaho Springs, CO 80452
(800) 876-6762
Ornabead.com
If you're looking for vintage-style clasps and beads, this is the place to check first.

Out on a Whim
121 E. Cotati Ave.
Cotati, CA 94931
(707) 664-8343
www.whimbeads.com
Seed beads in every color and finish imaginable and as far as the eye can see.

Soft Flex
PO Box 80
Sonoma, CA 95476
(866) 925-3539
www.softflexcompany.com
Top-quality beading wire, plus a great selection of tools, books, and precious and semiprecious stone beads. Check their site for really helpful design tips.

Thunderbird Supply Company
1907 W. Historic Route 66
Gallup, NM 87301-6612
(800) 545-7968
www.thunderbirdsupply.com
They have just about everything you need to bead, but their findings selection is especially stellar.

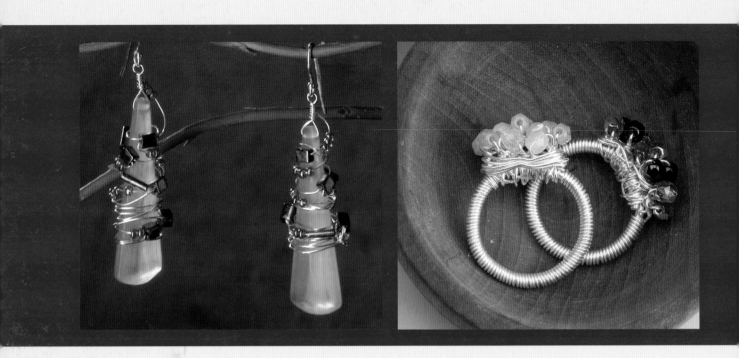

{Index}